素食
VEGETARIAN
COOKING

Chinese Style

編 著 者	財團法人味全文化教育基金會
烹飪製作	法華素食餐廳主廚　洪銀龍／洪銀國
	和平素食餐廳主廚　宋榮茂
	財團法人味全文化教育基金會家政班
出 版 者	純青出版社有限公司
	台北市松江路125號5樓
	郵政劃撥12106299
	電話：(02)5074902 . 5084331
著作財產權	財團法人味全文化教育基金會
版權所有	局版台業字第3884號
印　　刷	中華彩色印刷股份有限公司
	中華民國77年11月初版發行
	中華民國85年3月八版發行
	定價：新台幣參佰元整

Author	Lee Hwa Lin
Publisher	Chin Chin Publishing Co., Ltd.
	5th fl., 125, Sung Chiang Rd,
	Taipei, Taiwan, R.O.C.
	TEL:(02)5074902 . 5084331
Distributor	Wei-Chuan Publishing
	1455 Monterey Pass Rd, #110
	Monterey Park, CA 91754, U.S.A.
	TEL:(213)2613880 .2613878
	FAX:(213)2613299
	Printed in Taiwan, R.O.C.
Printer	China Color Printing Co., Inc.
Copyright Holder	Copyright © 1995
	By Wei-Chuan Cultural-Educational Foundation
	First Printing, November,1988
	Eighth Printing, June, 1996
	ISBN : 0-941676-20-X

序

　　健康的身體是人人渴望的，但要有好的身體，除了生活作息必須規律外，均衡的飲食也是必備條件。近年來，社會進步、經濟繁榮、物質豐富，人們所擔心的不再是「吃飽」問題，而是吃得太過豐富營養，出現種種現代病。在現代病比率愈來愈高下，各種病變也愈變愈可怕，更使人愈來愈重視「吃的技巧」。

　　過去人們認為只有出家人才吃齋，或是信佛的人在初一、十五吃素，都是把素食與宗教連在一起，而少有人把素食與健康銜接起來。甚至有人認為吃素食會面黃肌瘦，使得素食並不受人重視，如今社會形態改變，飲食習慣隨之變更。餐餐大魚大肉，比比皆是，各種疾病應運而生。現代醫學同時證明多吃素食，可減低血脂濃度，可預防心血管疾病，這使得吃素的人口益趨增多。

　　不可諱言的，早期的素食者，與宗教脫離不了關係，在宗教的素食中，葱、蒜、韭菜、洋葱、蕎頭代表「五葷」，而五葷是素食者的禁忌，在諸多調味品及材料的限制下，更使得素食變化少，很難滿足一般人口腹之慾，所以早些年長期吃素必須有毅力。

　　如今現代的醫學已證實多吃素菜對健康有益，博得追求健康者的重視。

　　味全文教基金會附設家政班針對這點，秉持服務大眾的一貫原則，編著「素食」食譜，並為了增加素食的美味，使社會大眾更能接受它，我們特地邀請法華餐廳的洪銀國、洪銀龍師傅及和平素食餐廳的宋榮茂師傅一起共同研究，如何使素菜更美味，經過長期慎重的鑽研終於完成了這本素食食譜。

　　在台灣，由於素食普遍，材料取得方面不成問題，但在國外就沒有這麼方便，因此本書的特色之一即是在第十三頁至十五頁有特殊材料之作法介紹，讓喜歡或需要自製「素材」的消費者，可以達到吃素的目的，另外在第十頁至十二頁有各種素食常用材料的圖片，使讀者在購買材料時更容易辨認材料。

　　最後我藉此再度謝謝幫助味全文教基金會完成此書的三位師傅，及所有味全家政班同仁。

FOREWORD

Good health is something everybody wants. In addition to sound and regular everyday habits, balanced nutrition is one of the most basic prerequisites to a healthy body. In recent years, one result of our rapidly advancing society, prosperous economy, and high material standard of living is concern not about getting enough to eat, but just the opposite. And one consequence of "overnutrition" has been a sharp rise in the incidence of all sorts of related modern illnesses. This phenomenon demands that we focus more closely on how and what we eat.

In China in the past, most people became vegetarians for purely religious reasons. People assumed that a vegetarian diet was of necessity nutritionally deficient and that vegetarians were all gaunt and weak, so for a long time vegetarianism did not receive much public attention. But as society has changed, so have our eating habits. Our consumption of meat and fish has increased greatly, and all sorts of chronic diseases have followed closely behind. Medical studies have proven that following a vegetarian diet can reduce the concentration of lipids in the blood, and lower the incidence of arterial sclerosis and other related ailments. This is an extra bonus to vegetarians.

Chinese vegetarianism is rooted firmly in Buddhist tradition. And formerly, not only was the consumption of meat and other flesh foods forbidden to Buddhists, but so were all forms of onion, garlic, chives, green onion, and *Allium chinense G. Don*. With all these restrictions of ingredients and seasonings, Chinese-style vegetarian food did not hold much appeal for the average layman, and anyone who chose a vegetarian lifestyle had to have a high degree of motivation and determination.

Now, however, in the face of undisputed evidence that vegetarianism is conducive to good health, more and more people are becoming vegetarians for health rather than religious reasons. In response to this trend, the Cooking School of the Wei-Chuan Cultural–Educational Foundation has compiled this book of "Vegetarian Cooking" as part of our ongoing service to our readers. The goal of this book is to promote Chinese vegetarian cooking by introducing our readers to a wide of variety of tempting, delicious, and original dishes. To this end, we invited master chefs Hung Yin-kuo and Hung Yin-lung of the Fa Hwa Vegetarian Restaurant and Sung Jung-mao of the Peace Vegetarian Restaurant to research ways of making Chinese vegetarian food even more tantalizing and tasty. The fruit of their painstaking efforts is this book of Chinese vegetarian cooking.

Because of the popularity of vegetarianism in Taiwan, special ingredients used in vegetarian dishes are widely available and easy to obtain. Outside of Taiwan, however, these ingredients are often not as easy to track down. Among the unique features of this book is a section found on pages 10 to 12 with descriptions and illustrations of the various special ingredients for Chinese vegetarian cooking, to help in identifying and buying them. And, for the ones your local Oriental grocery doesn't carry, pages 13 to 15 show you how to make them yourself at home.

Finally, I would like to take this opportunity to extend a special thanks to all those who assisted the Wei-Chuan Cultural-Educational Foundation in putting out this book, in particular, our team of three master chefs, and the entire staff of our Cooking School.

Lee Hwa Lin

食用素食・常保健康

　　由於美食及飽食，現代人不但爲肥胖而煩惱，更被心臟病、腦出血、糖尿病、癌症等成人病威脅到生命。在歐洲，於是流行素食，到處可看到素食餐館。

　　台灣這幾年來，各地的素食餐館、素食自助餐館也如雨後春筍般地出現。在裡面用膳的，除了宗教關係的人士以外，還有很多愛美麗的女性，以及關心自己健康的人士。

　　人類由草食進化爲雜食，這是在進化過程當中，人類學習肉食，發現肉食不但美味，更可給予精力及促進發育。不過很有趣的是，人類在這進化過程中，身體的許多生理作用並沒有很大的改變。

　　但由於加工食品等的流行，我們的胃腸以及新陳代謝，就面臨了無法適應的情況。這就是前述的成人病，以及便秘等煩惱，這都與不當的飲食有關係。

　　所謂不當的飲食，指的是偏食，或動物性食品吃得太多。愛斯基摩人群居於北極，由於地理環境的關係，他們以肉類爲主食，很少吃到蔬果類，依統計資料，他們平均壽命只有二十七歲，且大都患有神經痛等疾病，這是由於肉食過多所引起的毛病。

　　以上是對肉食所引起的問題加以說明，可是最重要的一點是，素食也是保持美容的最好辦法。素食可以讓女性身體的新陳代謝順暢，不會便秘，不會造成有害皮膚的胺類等化合物，可使皮膚有彈性，不粗糙而容光煥發。另外，重要的一點是，素食可使膽固醇降低，對患有成人病的人也有幫助。

　　不過站在營養學的立場，素食容易缺乏蛋白質，尤其是缺少良質的蛋白質。如果沒有宗教的約束，純素食者不妨也吃蛋類。至於牛奶以及奶製品都屬於素食，所以最好多喝牛奶，以及食用各種奶製品。

　　在素食中，豆類（尤其是黃豆、花生、芝麻等）麵筋以及其加工品含有良質的蛋白質，應多加以利用，以提高素食菜餚的營養平衡。

　　在餐館食用素食，雖然方便，但自己在家裡烹飪的菜餚，不但衛生安全，更含有親手做的感情。尤其是大家都注意健康的今天，希望能多食用素食來維持大家的美麗、健康、長壽。

李錦楓

VEGETARIANISM FOR HEALTH

Overweight is not the only popular concern in this age of plentiful and sophisticated food; heart disease, stroke, diabetes, cancer, and other adult diseases are some of the other threats we face today. Vegetarianism has thus become extremely popular in Europe and the United States, and vegetarian restaurants have opened up practically everywhere in response.

In recent years, vegetarian restaurants have also become a common sight in Taiwan. Besides those who eat in such establishments for religious reasons, more and more people now patronize them for physical health and beauty.

In the process of evolving from herbivore to omnivore, the human race learned to eat meat. Man discovered that flesh foods were not only tasty, but also provided him with energy and accelerated growth. It is notable, however, that in the evolutionary process, most of the original physiological functions of the body did not change along with the change in diet.

Now, in this age of processed foods, our digestive systems and metabolisms are facing a crisis of adjustment they cannot cope with. One result of this crisis is the series of adult diseases just mentioned, along with constipation and other ailments related to an inappropriate diet.

An "inappropriate diet" is one that is either lopsided toward one particular kind of food, or that includes too many meat and flesh foods. Due to the limitations of their environment, Eskimos living in the Arctic Circle consume mainly flesh foods and rarely eat vegetables. According to statistics, their average life expectancy is only 27 years, and most suffer from neural disorders and other related ailments. This can be traced to eating too much flesh food.

Another significant benefit of a vegetarian diet is that it promotes beauty. A vegetarian diet stimulates the metabolism and makes for a smoothly functioning digestive system, and it prevents constipation and damage to the skin resulting from the formation of amine and other harmful compounds. It makes the skin more supple, smooth, and glowing. Adhering to a vegetarian diet can also lower cholesterol count, an important benefit for those suffering from a variety of adult diseases.

One thing to guard against is inadequate intake of the complete proteins our bodies need. If free from religious restrictions, vegetarians should include eggs in their diet. Milk and dairy products are high-protein vegetarian foods that all vegetarians should get plenty of to insure good nutrition.

Other vegetarian foods that are high in complete proteins are beans and legumes (especially soy beans, peanuts, sesame seed, and so forth) and wheat gluten, and products made from them. Vegetarians should eat plenty of these foods for balanced and complete nutrition.

Eating vegetarian food in a restaurant is certainly convenient, but when cooking your own vegetarian dishes you can control the sanitary conditions, and add a home-cooked touch to your meals that no restaurant could ever match. In this age of health and beauty consciousness, vegetarianism is one good way to cultivate both.

Chin Feng Li

佛教的素食觀

　　我吃全素到現在已經有四年多的時間了，剛吃素的時候，許多親戚朋友都爲我擔心，因爲在一般人的觀念裡，總認爲素食的營養不夠，而且在現代社會人人以魚肉是尚，吃素是非常不方便的。另外，老一輩的中國人非常相信熱補，總覺得素食裡的豆類、青菜、蘿蔔都是「性冷」，吃了不能補身，也就是説，認爲素食不補，要虎鞭、蛇血、燉雞、醉蟹這些東西才補。

　　在立下吃素的願望時，我就不在乎營養是不是夠、吃飯是不是方便、素食是不是補的問題，因爲我的素食動機與這些毫無關係，我是由於佛教的信仰才吃素的。

　　佛教爲什麼主張素食呢？主要是爲了「慈悲」，是爲了「不忍食衆生肉」。其次，是爲了深信因果，依佛所教，一刀一命所造的惡因，在受報時是絕對不會落空的，佛經裡説「菩薩畏因、衆生畏果」，是説菩薩不造惡因，是知道果的可怕，而衆生迷迷糊糊的過日子，造下許多惡因，他們只害怕苦果，卻很少想到苦果的原因。最後，是爲了「清淨」，我深信素食者較容易身心清淨，而身心清淨是修行的一個很重要的基本。我的素食也是由這三個觀點出發。

　　關於慈悲，是佛最重要的教化，沒有慈悲心的人根本不配稱爲佛的弟子。慈悲心當然可以從生活的各處顯現出來，但是最直接最簡單的表達沒有比吃素更好的了。想一想，我們走路時不小心踩到一支釘子都會痛得死去活來，我們桌上的衆生之肉，要經過被宰殺、剝皮、肢解、烹煮的痛苦，怎麼能忍心下筷子呢？當我們不忍心下筷子時，就是慈悲心油然的流露。

　　我説衆生的肉被端上餐桌要歷經許多痛苦，絕非虛言，就以現代人最愛吃的活煮蝦蟹來説，在熱鍋中活燒而死的蝦蟹，就有如經過了地獄裡的沸湯大獄，牠們在裡面痛苦的爬行跳躍不能解脱，最後含恨而亡，全身盡赤，這是多麼痛苦的煎熬！

　　蟹蝦還不是最痛苦的，以市場上的青蛙爲例，一隻青蛙從被殺一直到吞進人的腹中，經歷猶如受八種地獄之苦：1.斷頭地獄。2.剝皮地獄。3.落足地獄（去掉四隻腳爪）。4.剖腹地獄（挖空內臟）。5.沸油地獄（或炒或煮）。6.鹹糟地獄（調和五味）。7.磕石地獄（牙齒咬嚙）。8.糞尿地獄（流入腸胃直到排出）。若能把自己觀想成一隻蛙，稍有心腸的人就吃不下去。

　　人間集體的痛苦裡，最甚的莫過於刀兵的劫難，我們看南京大屠殺或納粹殺猶太人的影片資料，很少人能不動容落淚、義憤填膺。可是刀兵劫在人間可能數年、數十年才有一次，而在畜牲道裡則是無日無之，對於吃葷的人，每次辦一桌酒席，屠殺的衆生何止千百，這不是一次刀兵的劫難嗎？

　　爲了衆生不因我們的口腹之慾而受難，實是最起碼的慈悲心，以慈心故，所以不殺；以悲心故，所以不食。

　　有兩個有關慈悲的故事，我讀過後非常感動，永不能忘。一個記載在「護生錄」裡：

　　學士周豫，煮鱔魚時，看見有一條鱔魚的身體弓起，以頭尾就沸湯中，腹部則彎起立於湯外，至死都不倒下。周豫覺得非常奇怪，把那條鱔魚撈起來剖開，發現腹中原來有魚卵無數，爲了護子而彎身避開湯水，他看了惻然淚下，感慨不已，發誓永不食鱔。

　　這故事告訴我們，衆生不是無情無識，也不是無知無感的。

　　另一則記載在「起世因本經」裡：

　　忉利天的天王與阿修羅作戰，雙方打得難分難解、不分勝負。天王領兵而返時，看見路旁大樹有金翅鳥巢，心想：「若帶兵過此，巢中鳥蛋必被車馬震落。」遂令千輛戰車折返原路。阿修羅看見帝釋回轉，心中驚怖，大潰而逃。

　　經典上的結論是「以慈力故，帝釋得勝。」這個故事告訴我們，慈悲看起來好像沒有什麼，其實有極大的力量，佛經上常用「慈悲力」，可見慈悲的力量很大。佛教徒要發揮慈悲的力量，就要學帝釋一樣，寧可千輛戰車換路而行，不忍心震落一窩鳥蛋。

楞嚴經裡說：「食衆生肉，斷大悲種。」積極的說，不吃衆生的肉，就是在培養灌漑大悲心的種子，一個人不吃葷食，慈悲心自然會長養出來，爲了「不斷大悲種」、爲了「長養慈悲心」，我選擇素食，而且這是最重要的理由。

其次，關於因果。佛教的因果說法固然千變萬化，但是它的基本觀念很簡單，就是「善有善報、惡有惡報；不是不報、時候未到」。若從這個觀念出發，我們吃衆生的一塊肉，將來必有一塊肉之報；我們殺衆生一條命，將來必有一條命之報。若從長遠處看來，吃衆生肉是一件多麼可怕的事，衆生臨死之前沒有歡喜的，不是恐懼、就是憤怒；不是含怨，就是懷恨；這些要報在誰的身上呢？

因果難以考證，想起來也蠻遙遠。就以今生來說，食肉也要受惡果，醫學界已發現像血管粥狀硬化、心臟病、高血壓、腦充血、中風、膽結石、肝硬化、癌症都與動物油脂及膽固醇有密切關係。所以，吃葷的因果歷歷在目，既然同樣都可以過日子，又對健康有益，還不必擔心將來的因果問題，爲什麼不茹素呢？這是我決定素食的第二個理由。

我吃素的第三個理由是想要使「身心清淨」，這一點似乎有些費解。美國有一位素食醫生說得最好：「在吃飯時，不必擔心你所吃的食物是死於何種疾病眞是一件好事。」這指出了通常動物不是百分之百健康的，臨死前還會分化出毒素，我們吃了動物的肉，無疑也吃下這些疾病與毒素。

根據「大英百科全書」記載，身體中的毒素，包括尿酸與其他有毒的排泄物，會出現在血液與身體組織內，因此提出了中肯的見解:「若是與牛肉中所含的百分之六十五不淨的水分相比較，從堅果、豆類及穀類中所得到的蛋白質，顯然要純淨多了。」素食確實比肉類清潔，也比肉類容易保持新鮮，在素食中與肉類相同的營養成分裡，每一樣都比肉類乾淨、純粹。我們知道，肉類是很容易敗壞的，魚蝦類半小時就開始有異味，而肉品則在一小時就開始腐化了，素食則無此弊，一般菜蔬放個三、五天絕無問題，豆類雖容易酸壞，卻極易辨別。

現代的素食縱使有農藥之弊，但比起肉食是乾淨得多，一個人常吃清淨的食物，身心較能處在清淨的狀態，這是理所當然、事所必致，無可懷疑的。

還有一個素食者常被問起的問題，就是爲什麼葱、韭菜、洋葱、大蒜不能吃呢？這也與清淨有關，「楞嚴經」講：「諸衆生求三摩提，當斷世間五種辛食。此五種辛，熟食發淫，生啖增恚。」又說：「如是世間食辛之人，縱能宣說十二部經，十方天仙嫌其臭穢，咸皆遠離。」意思是說，五辛會使人起淫念、脾氣暴躁、身體臭穢，這些都是不清淨的，一個人身心不能清淨，修清淨法怎麼可能成功呢？這就是爲什麼「大乘入楞伽經」要這樣說的道理：「夫血肉者，衆仙所棄，群聖不食……夫食肉者，諸天遠離，口氣常臭……，肉非美好，肉不清淨，生諸罪惡，敗諸功德，諸仙聖人之所棄捨！」

這些年來，我很少把心思放在吃東西上面，吃素的心得其實很少，不過，這三個理由已經使我覺得理直氣壯，至於吃素是不是更有營養、是不是有什麼功德、是不是能增進世界和平，眞的是「猶其餘事」耳！

我所堅信的是，一個人要學佛、要進入佛的慈悲與智慧，必須要先從餐桌做起。英國有一位提倡素食的華爾緒博士，曾說過一句名言：「要想避免人類流血，便須從餐桌上做起。」放眼今日台灣，食則一席千命，衣則貂皮蠶絲，履則鱷皮牛革，淫則倚翠偎紅，這樣的地方要在餐桌上悟得慈悲、因果、清淨的智慧，似乎蠻艱難的，此地長久的平安富足想起來就令人憂心了。

A BUDDHIST
VIEW OF VEGETARIANISM

I have been a strict vegetarian for more than four years now. When I first gave up meat, quite a few of my friends and relatives expressed concern; most people seem to have the idea that vegetarian food lacks adequate nutrients. And being vegetarian can be a more than minor inconvenience with the amounts of meat and fish that people now eat. Chinese have a traditional notion that foods that are "warming" in nature, like meat, are important for building up physical strength; so in the minds of some of the older generation, one could not possibly get all the nutrition one needed from the "cool" beans, greens, white radishes, and so forth that vegetarians favor. In their book, the only things that can strengthen the body are foods like tiger phallus, snake blood, stewed chicken, and crab in wine.

Before taking the big step, I didn't give nutrition, convenience, or building up physical strength a second thought, since my reason for becoming vegetarian had nothing to do with any of these. I became vegetarian because of my belief in Buddhism.

Why do Buddhists advocate vegetarianism? The main reason is "mercy," and because we "cannot bear to eat the flesh of living creatures." And our belief in karma tells us that we must eventually suffer the consequences of our evil actions. A Buddhist sutra says: "The bodhisattva fears the original action; the myriad living creatures fear the consequences." This means that the bodhisattva knows the seriousness of the consequences and does not do evil things; neither does he think about the causes of bad consequences. Finally, I also believe that a vegetarian diet better enables one to keep a pure body and mind; and this purity is an important foundation of self-cultivation. My conversion to vegetarianism was based on these three considerations.

"Mercy" is an important way of learning to be a better person. Being without mercy is simply incompatible with being a Buddhist. Having a merciful and compassionate heart will show up in all aspects of one's life; but the simplest and most direct way is to follow a vegetarian diet. Think of how intense the pain of accidentally stepping on a nail is. So how can one have the heart to eat the flesh of creatures who have suffered the pain of being slaughtered, skinned, dismembered, and cooked? Being unable to bring ourselves to eat the flesh of these poor creatures is an expression of mercy.

The pain of creatures on the road to our table is not some fanciful concoction; it is excruciatingly real. Let us cite the cooked live shrimp and crab that are so popular today as an example. Meeting their end by being cooked in water is like being sent to a boiling hell. Their desperate but doomed efforts to crawl or jump out betray the unbearable pain they experience. Finally they give up their life in sorrow as they turn bright red. What a painful end!

Frogs are put through even more suffering than shrimp and crabs. From the first cut made in their bodies to the time they are swallowed, they go through the equivalent of eight different hells: 1. decapitation; 2. skinning; 3. removing the legs; 4. slitting of the belly; 5. frying or boiling; 6. salt, sugar and seasoning; 7. chewing; and 8. digestion and excretion. Anyone who put himself in the place of a frog would be unable to ever stomach another one.

Among the different kinds of suffering the human race can experience, the most intense is certainly that of war. Documentaries of the Nanking massacre and the Nazi holocaust leave few people unmoved and dry-eyed—and most indignant. But humans can go for years or decades without war; animals face suffering and death every day. For meat-eaters, every banquet means the death of hundreds and thousands of animals. Is this any different from human war?

Preventing suffering of living creatures by not using their flesh to satisfy our tastebuds and hunger is the minimal expression of compassion we can offer. We choose not to kill out of kindness, and not to eat out of compassion.

I felt deeply moved upon reading two stories on the theme of mercy; they will be etched forever in my memory. One is recorded in the book, "Record of Protecting Life":

When a scholar named Chou Yu was cooking some eel to eat, he noticed one of the eels bending its body such that its head and tail were still in the boiling liquid, but its body arched upward above the soup. It did not fall completely in until finally dying. Chou Yu found the occurrence a strange one, pulled out the eel, and cut it open. He found thousands of eggs inside. The eel had arched its belly out of the hot soup to protect its offspring. He cried at the sight, sighed with emotion, and swore never again to eat eel.

This story tells us that the myriad living creatures are not without feeling and intelligence. Another story is recorded in a Buddhist sutra:

A king of heaven was stalemated in a war with a demon, and neither side emerged as winner. As the king of heaven was leading his solidiers back, he saw the nest of a golden-winged bird in a tree by the roadside. "If soldiers and chariots pass by here, the eggs in the nest will certainly fall to the ground and be scattered," he thought to himself. So he led his thousand chariots back the same road by which they came. When the demon saw the king of heaven returning, he fled in terror.

The sutra's conclusion was that "if you use mercy to seek salvation, the lord of heaven will see it." This story tells us that mercy may not seem like much at first glance, but it is in fact extremely powerful. The Buddhist sutras frequently mention "the power of mercy;" from this we know that mercy is indeed a potent force. If a Buddhist wants to learn to use this strength of mercy, he must be like the king of heaven in this story, and be ready to change the route of a thousand chariots rather than let a nest full of bird eggs fall to the ground.

The Śūrāṅgama Sutra tells us that "if we eat the flesh of living creatures, we are destroying the seeds of compassion." That is, if we do not eat the flesh of living creatures, we are cultivating and irrigating the seeds of great compassion. A compassionate heart will naturally be cultivated in a person who does not eat meat. So, to "avoid destroying the seeds of compassion," and to "cultivate a compassionate heart," I chose to become a vegetarian; and this is my main reason for doing so.

In Buddhist teaching, volume upon volume has been written regarding cause and consequence, but the basic concept is a simple one. "Good is rewarded with good; evil is rewarded with evil; and the rewarding of good and evil is only a matter of time." Viewed from this concept, we will have to pay for every piece of flesh we eat with a piece of flesh, and with a life for every creature's life that we take. Viewed over the long term, eating meat is an extremely frightening prospect. Before their death, living creatures experience not joy, and not fear, but anger; not complaint, but hatred and resentment. And who receives the "reward" for taking these lives?

It would be difficult to try to prove the existence of this concept of cause and consequence, and it may even sound a bit farfetched. However, in terms of this life, the negative consequences of eating meat include arterial sclerosis, heart disease, high blood pressure, encephalemia, stroke, gall stones, cirrhosis of the liver, and cancer. In all of these diseases, a link has been established to animal fat and cholesterol. So the consequences of eating meat are in fact immediate and in clear view. But even if you could still make it from day to day eating meat, the other advantages of being vegetarian—promotion of good health and being free from worry about future negative consequences—to me fully justify the decision to be vegetarian, and constitute my second main reason for doing so.

My third reason is to "purify body and mind." This one might seem to escape logical explanation. An American vegetarian physician summed it up well when he said that "It's good not having to worry about the conditions under which your food died." This statement points out that animals are not always healthy themselves, and before death, they secrete toxic substances. When we eat the flesh of animals, we also ingest disease-carrying microorganisms and toxins.

According to the Encyclopaedia Britannica, our bodies contain uric acid and other toxic waste products which turn up in our blood and body tissues. Compared to the 65 percent impure moisture content of beef, protein obtained from nuts, beans, and legumes is markedly purer. Vegetarian food is indeed much cleaner than meat, and it also retains its freshness better than meat. Vegetarian food is in every case cleaner and purer than meat with comparable nutritious value. We know that meat spoils easily, and fish and shrimp begin to become putrid after being left out for just half an hour. Meat and meat products begin to decay after one hour. Vegetables, on the other hand, can usually be kept for three to five days. Although beans become rancid relatively quickly, the deterioration is very easy to detect and recognize.

One problem with vegetable foods today is contamination by pesticides; but even so, they are still much cleaner than meat. A person who habitually eats pure food keeps his body and mind in a pure state; this follows of course, and is beyond argument.

Another question that vegetarians are frequently asked is, "Why can't you eat scallions, chives, onions, and garlic?" This again relates back to purity. The Śūraṅgama Sutra says: "All living creatures seek the 'three kinds of wisdom,' and should refrain from eating the 'five pungent foods.' These five pungent foods create lust when eaten cooked, and rage when eaten raw." It goes on to say that "Even if someone can recite twelve sutras from memory, the gods of the ten heavens will all disdain him if he eats pungent foods in this world, because of his strong odor and uncleanliness, and will distance themselves far from him." This means that pungent foods arouse lust, and give one an explosive temper and one's body a bad odor. These foods are unclean, and if a person's body and mind are not clean, how can he succeed at purifying himself through Buddhism? This is why yet another sutra says: "That which has blood and flesh will be rejected by the gods and not eaten by the saints; all in heaven distance themselves far from one who eats meat; his breath is always foul...meat is not a good thing, meat is not pure, it is born in evil and spoils in merit and virtue; it is rejected by all the gods and saints!"

In recent years, I have not spent much time thinking about what I eat; in fact, I don't have many great insights on vegetarianism. However, the three reasons I just stated are sufficient to make me feel confident about my choice. Issues like whether a vegetarian diet is more nutritious, whether there is great merit in following a vegetarian diet, whether it can promote world peace, and so forth, are all secondary.

What I strongly believe is that if a person wants to take joy in the Buddhist way and enter into the mercy and knowledge of the Buddha, he must begin at the dining table. There is a British promoter of vegetarianism named Dr. Walsh who once said that "To prevent human bloodshed one must start at the dinner table." Turning back to Taiwan today, one banquet takes a thousand lives; clothing oneself requires minks and silk spun by worms; shoes are made from alligator skin and leather; and lust and luxury are carried to extremes. To begin one's enlightenment of mercy and cause and consequence at the dinner table in this kind of an environment is perhaps more than a little difficult. The prospects for long-term peace and prosperity here are indeed cause for concern.

Lin Ching-Shyuan

干 瓢 dried gourd shavings
(kampyō)

素肉片 vegetarian pork slices

扁 尖 dried bamboo shoots

蓮 子 lotus seeds

當 歸 Chinese angelica
(tang kuei)

白 果 gingko nuts

麵筋泡 wheat gluten puffs

枸 杞 Chinese wolfberry seeds
(kou chi tzu)

紅 棗 dried Chinese red dates

竹 笙 bamboo pith

麵 輪 wheat gluten wheels

黃 茸 edible yellow fungus
(huang jung)

素排骨 vegetarian ribs

油　條 Chinese fried cruller
(you-tiao)

金　針 dried lily buds

蓮　藕 lotus root

黃豆沙 yellow mung bean paste

栗　子 dried chestnuts

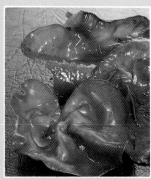

木　耳 wood ears
(edible tree fungus)

素　肚 vegetarian tripe

芥藍菜 Chinese kale
(*kailan choi*)

蒟蒻 *konnyaku*

豆　豉 fermented black beans

乾粉皮 dried mung bean sheets

麵 腸 wheat gluten sausage

桔 餅 candied kumquats

冬瓜糖 winter melon candy

豆 包 bean curd pockets

黑豆干 dark pressed bean curd

烤 麩 bran puffs

白豆干 white pressed bean curd

豆 皮 bean curd skin

百 頁 bean curd sheets
(pai yeh)

鍋 耙 crisp rice cakes
(kuo pa)

白豆支 dried pressed bean curd
strips

桂 皮 stick cinnamon

素魚 Vegetarian Fish

材料：

豆包⋯⋯⋯⋯⋯⋯⋯ 200公克	玉米粉⋯⋯⋯⋯⋯⋯ 1大匙
金菇、荸薺⋯⋯⋯⋯各80公克	② 塩、味精⋯⋯⋯⋯各¼小匙
豆皮、紫菜⋯⋯⋯⋯各 1張	胡椒粉⋯⋯⋯⋯⋯⋯¼小匙
① 麵粉⋯⋯⋯⋯⋯⋯ 1大匙	蛋⋯⋯⋯⋯⋯⋯⋯⋯1個
水⋯⋯⋯⋯⋯⋯⋯ 1大匙	

❶①料調勻成麵糊，豆包、荸薺切末，金菇洗淨去頭切末與②料拌勻成餡均備用。

❷ 1張豆皮上放紫菜1張，餡1份(圖一)，再捲成10×6公分之長方塊(圖二)，接口以麵糊粘緊，入蒸籠以大火蒸30分鐘，取出是爲素魚。

INGREDIENTS:

200 g (7 oz.)	bean curd pockets
80 g (3 oz.) each:	*enoki*, water chestnuts
1 sheet each:	bean curd skin, purple laver seaweed
① { 1 T.	flour
1 T.	water
② { 1 T.	cornstarch
¼ t. each:	salt, pepper
1	egg

❶ Mix ① into a smooth batter. Mince the bean curd pockets and the water chestnuts. Wash the *enoki*, trim off the ends, and mince. Mix the minced ingredients with ② until well blended. This is the filling.

❷ Place the purple laver on top of the bean curd skin, then place the filling on top of the purple laver (illus. 1). Roll into a 10×6 cm (4″×2½″) rectangular block (illus. 2). Seal tightly with the batter. Steam 30 minutes over high heat. Use this wherever "vegetarian fish" is called for.

❶

❷

素魷魚 Vegetarian Squid

材料：

蒟蒻粉⋯⋯⋯⋯⋯⋯10公克	① 鹼粉⋯⋯⋯⋯⋯⋯ 5公克
小黃瓜⋯⋯⋯⋯⋯⋯ 2條	紅蘿蔔汁⋯⋯⋯⋯⋯¾杯
白布⋯⋯⋯⋯⋯⋯⋯ 2條	

❶蒟蒻粉與①料拌勻成糰，分成2等份備用。

❷小黃瓜1條以1份❶料包裹(圖一)，再以白布包緊，另1份作法亦同，入蒸籠以大火蒸至熟約20分鐘，取出，將布拿掉，再以刀子在中間劃一刀(圖二)，取出小黃瓜即爲素魷魚。

■素海參與素魷魚的作法相同，將①料之紅蘿蔔汁改爲水即可。

INGREDIENTS:

10 g (⅓ oz.)	*konnyaku* powder
2	gherkin cucumbers
2 strips	white cloth
① { 1½ t. (⅙ oz.)	baking soda
¾ c.	carrot juice

❶ Mix the *konnyaku* powder with ① to form a dough, and divide into two equal portions.

❷ Cover the outside of each gherkin cucumber with the *konnyaku* dough from step ①, then wrap each in a strip of clean white cloth. Steam over high heat until done, about 20 minutes. Remove the white cloth, then make a slash down each with a knife (illus. 2). Remove the gherkin cucumber. This is the "vegetarian cuttlefish."

Note: The method for making vegetarian sea cucumber is the same as for vegetarian cuttlefish; except use plain water instead of carrot juice in ①.

❶

❷

素烏魚子 Vegetarian Fish Roe

材料：

鹹蛋黃	8個		起士粉	1大匙
圓形模型	1個	①	太白粉	2小匙
油	1小匙		塩、味精	各¼小匙

❶將鹹蛋黃壓碎，入①料拌勻（圖一）。

❷圓形模型抹油，將蛋黃倒入模型（圖二）內，入蒸籠以大火蒸10分鐘，取出待冷倒扣，即爲成品。

INGREDIENTS:

8		yolks of Chinese salted duck eggs
1		small rectangular cake pan
1 t.		oil
	1 T.	grated Parmesan cheese
①	2 T.	cornstarch
	¼ t.	salt

❶ Mash the yolks of the salted duck eggs, and mix in ① until thoroughly blended.

❷ Oil the small cake pan, then pour the mashed egg yolk mixture into it (illus. 1). Steam 10 minutes over high heat. Remove from the steamer and allow to cool. Invert onto a plate (illus. 2). Use in recipes calling for vegetarian fish roe.

素鷄 Vegetarian Chicken

材料：

百頁	20張		水	2杯
白布	1條		醬油膏	1大匙
炸油	6杯		番茄醬	1大匙
①{ 鹼塊	¼小塊	③	味精、胡椒 ├	1小匙
水	4杯		糖	1小匙
②{ 水	3杯		八角	4個
塩	1大匙		薑	3片

❶百頁每張均切2×2公分小塊，入①料以中火煮5分鐘即撈起，再入②料以中火續煮5分鐘，撈起、瀝乾，趁熱用白布包成10×6×2公分之長方塊（圖一），包好後以重物壓2小時（圖二）備用。

❷炸油燒8分熱（約350°F），將壓好之百頁取出油炸成金黃色後，取出瀝油，再入③料以小火滷10分鐘，取出待涼切片排盤即成。

INGREDIENTS:

20		bean curd sheets (pai yeh)
1 strip		white cloth
6 c.		oil for frying
①	1 t.	baking soda
	4 c.	water
②	3 c.	water
	1 T.	salt
	2 c.	water
	1 T. each:	thick soy sauce, ketchup
③	1 t. each:	pepper, sugar,
	4 flowerets	star anise
	3 slices	ginger root

❶ Cut each bean curd sheet into 2×2 cm (¾" × ¾") squares. Add ① and cook 5 minutes over medium heat. Remove from the liquid. Cook another 5 minutes over medium heat together with ②, then again remove from the liquid. Drain. While still hot, wrap in the white cloth into a 10×6×2 cm (4"×2½"×¾") rectangular block (illus. 1). Place under a weight for 2 hours (illus. 2).

❷ Heat the oil to about 350°F (177°C). Remove the cloth and fry the pressed bean curd sheets until golden. Drain well. Cook in ③ 10 minutes over low heat to season. Remove from the liquid, allow to cool, and slice. Arrange on a plate and serve.

素火腿 Vegetarian Ham

材料：

豆腐皮······10張	白芝麻······1大匙
年糕紙······1張	醬油······1大匙
棉繩······1條 ①	糖、味精······各½小匙
	麻油······½小匙
	五香粉······少許

❶豆腐皮切絲，入①料醃10分鐘後，以年糕紙包捲成長條狀（圖一），是爲素火腿。

❷將捲好的素火腿以棉繩綁緊（圖二），入蒸籠以大火蒸40分鐘，待涼取下棉繩及年糕紙再切片即成。

INGREDIENTS:

10 sheets	bean curd skin
1 sheet	cellophane
1 length	cotton string
① 1 T. each:	white sesame seeds, soy sauce
½ t. each:	sugar, sesame oil
pinch	Chinese five-spice powder

❶ Cut the bean curd skin into julienne strips. Marinate 10 minutes in ①. Wrap in the cellophane, forming a long cylindrical shape (illus. 1). This is the "vegetarian ham."

❷ Tie the vegetarian ham tightly with the string (illus. 2). Steam 40 minutes over high heat. Allow to cool, then remove the string and the cellophane. Slice and serve.

素高湯 Vegetarian Stock

材料：

黃豆芽······300公克
水······600公克

黃豆芽洗淨，與水入鍋中煮沸後，改小火慢慢熬，待湯汁剩一半時，即將黃豆芽撈出，再將湯汁過濾，即爲素高湯。

■1.素高湯的作法有許多種，此道食譜爲本書所用之素高湯作法。

2.一般素食之香味以香菇爲主，所以在紅燒方面的高湯以香菇頭、黃豆芽、紅蘿蔔皮、白蘿蔔皮及大白菜的老葉熬成高湯。

3.清炒之清高湯則以大白菜之老葉、黃豆芽、紅蘿蔔皮、白蘿蔔皮、芹菜葉熬成高湯。

INGREDIENTS:

300 g (⅔ lb.)   soy bean sprouts
600 g (1⅓ lb.)   water

Wash the soy bean sprouts, place them in a pot with the water, and bring to a boil. Lower the heat and allow to simmer. When only half the original volume of liquid remains, remove the soy bean sprouts and strain the broth.

❶ There are many different ways of making vegetarian stock. This recipe is the one referred to in this book wherever vegetarian stock is called for.

❷ Many Chinese vegetarian dishes rely on dried Chinese black mushrooms for flavor; so dried Chinese black mushroom stems, soy bean sprouts, carrot and Chinese white radish peelings, and the wilted outer leaves of Chinese cabbage can be added to vegetarian stock to be used in soy-simmered dishes.

❸ For stir-fried dishes or clear soups, use vegetarian stock made with the wilted outer leaves of Chinese cabbage, soy bean sprouts, carrot and Chinese white radish peelings, and celery leaves.

目錄 Contents

煮類 Simmered Dishes

湯類 Soups

點心類 Snacks and Sweets

花式拼盤

Flower Platter

材料：

素火腿	150公克		水	1杯
素烏魚子	100公克		醬油	1小匙
素排骨	100公克	①	番茄醬	¾小匙
紅蘿蔔	60公克		糖、味精	⅓小匙
大黃瓜	60公克		塩	¾小匙
蘆筍紫捲	3條		糖	¾小匙
香菇	3朵		醋	¾小匙
番茄(切片)	2個	②	麻油	¾小匙
生菜葉	4片		胡椒粉	少許
白蘿蔔花	1朵			
炸油	4杯			

❶香菇泡軟去蒂入①料，以小火滷約10分鐘，待湯汁收乾即成滷香菇。將滷香菇瀝乾，切約1公分寬之斜片(圖一)中央先放一片，再左右交疊排成花瓣狀(圖二)，並修去邊緣不齊的部份(圖三)，置於盤子外圈備用。

❷紅蘿蔔、大黃瓜均切2×5公分薄片，以¾小匙塩抓軟後，用水沖去塩份，再入②料醃10分鐘後瀝乾備用。

❸炸油燒7分熱(約300°F)，將素烏魚子炸香撈起，待涼後與素排骨均切成2×5公分之薄片備用。

❹❷及❸料依香菇片之排法，各排成大黃瓜花瓣，紅蘿蔔花瓣，排骨花瓣，素烏魚子花瓣，將此四個花瓣置於盤子外圈與香菇花瓣組合成五花瓣之花形，備用。

❺素火腿切2×5公分之厚片，蘆筍紫捲切約4公分長段備用。

❻將番茄片、素火腿片、蘆筍紫捲依先後次序，各排一圈在花形之中央，最後在蘆筍紫捲上置生菜及白蘿蔔花裝飾即成。

INGREDIENTS:

150 g (⅓ lb.)		vegetarian (bean curd) ham
100 g (3½ oz.)		vegetarian fish roe
100 g (3½ oz.)		vegetarian pork ribs
60 g (2 oz.)		carrot
60 g (2 oz.)		cucumber
3		asparagus-seaweed rolls
3		dried Chinese black mushrooms
2		tomatoes, sliced
4		lettuce leaves
1		Chinese white radish, carved into a flower
4 c.		oil for frying
①	1 c.	water
	1 t.	soy sauce
	¾ t.	ketchup
	⅓ t.	sugar
	¾ t.	salt
②	¾ t.	sugar
	¾ t.	rice vinegar
	¾ t.	sesame oil
	pinch	pepper

❶ Soak the dried mushrooms until soft, remove the stems, and simmer in ① over low heat about 10 minutes, until the sauce is cooked almost dry. These are "soy-seasoned mushrooms." Drain the mushrooms and cut diagonally into slices about 1 cm (⅓") wide (illus. 1). First place one slice in the center, then stack more strips on the left and right, overlapping to form a petal shape (illus. 2). Trim any uneven edges (illus. 3). Place near the rim of the serving platter.

❷ Cut the carrot and cucumber into 2×5 cm (¾"×2") thin slices. Rub in ¾ teaspoon salt to soften, then rinse with water to remove the salt. Add ② and allow to marinate for 10 minutes. Drain.

❸ Heat the oil for frying to about 300°F (149°C). Deep-fry the vegetarian fish roe until fragrant and remove from the oil. Allow to cool, then cut the vegetarian fish roe and the vegetarian pork ribs into 2×5 cm (¾"×2") thin slices.

❹ Arrange the ingredients in steps ❷ and ❸ as you did the mushroom strips, forming carrot, cucumber, vegetarian pork rib, and vegetarian fish roe petals. Arrange near the rim of the serving platter into a 5-petal flower pattern.

❺ Cut the vegetarian ham into 2×5 cm (¾"×2") thick slices. Cut the asparagus-seaweed rolls into 4 cm (1½") lengths.

❻ Arrange the tomato slices, the vegetarian ham slices, and the asparagus-seaweed rolls, in this order, in a circle in the center of the flower pattern. Finally, add the lettuce leaves and the white radish flower on top of the asparagus rolls as a garnish. Serve.

蝴蝶拼盤 / Butterfly Platter

材料：

素排骨	150公克	櫻桃、青豆仁	各2個
素火腿	150公克	塩	1小匙
素烏魚子	100公克	炸油	4杯
小黃瓜	100公克	① 糖	1小匙
紅蘿蔔	100公克	醋	1小匙
馬鈴薯	50公克	麻油	1小匙
滷香菇(作法見花式拼盤)		胡椒粉	少許
	4朵		

❶馬鈴薯去皮、煮熟、壓成泥，捏成10公分長條狀備用。

❷取1朵滷香菇依其形狀剪成2條約1公分寬10公分長之條狀(圖一)爲蝴蝶鬚，另3朵切1公分寬片狀，中央先放1片再左右交疊排成花瓣狀(如花式拼盤之圖二)，並修去邊緣不齊的部份，覆蓋在馬鈴薯泥上(圖二)，成蝴蝶之身體。

❸紅蘿蔔去皮，與小黃瓜均切2×5公分之薄片，以1小匙的塩抓軟後用水沖去塩份，再以①料醃10分鐘後瀝乾備用。

❹炸油燒至7分熱(約300°F)，將素烏魚子炸香撈起，待涼後與素火腿、素排骨均切成2×5公分之薄片備用。

❺❸及❹料依香菇片之排法，各排成2個素排骨花瓣、紅蘿蔔花瓣、小黃瓜花瓣及1個素烏魚子花瓣、火腿花瓣。取一排骨花瓣、火腿花瓣置於蝴蝶左邊，其上各放一小黃瓜花瓣及紅蘿蔔花瓣(圖三)此爲蝴蝶之左翼，剩餘4片花瓣以同樣方法排於右翼，最後以1個櫻桃對切，及2個青豆仁裝飾成蝴蝶之眼睛即成。

INGREDIENTS:

150 g (⅓ lb.)	vegetarian pork ribs
150 g (⅓ lb.)	vegetarian ham
100 g (3½ oz.)	vegetarian fish roe
100 g (3½ oz.)	gherkin cucumber
100 g (3½ oz.)	carrot
50 g (1¾ oz.)	potato
4	soy-seasoned Chinese black mushrooms (see *Flower Platter* p. 21)
2 each:	maraschino cherries, peas
1 t.	salt
4 c.	oil for frying
① 1 t.	sugar
1 t.	rice vinegar
1 t.	sesame oil
pinch	pepper

❶ Pare the potatoes, boil until cooked through, and mash. Form into a 10 cm (4″) long mound and set aside.

❷ Cut a soy-seasoned Chinese black mushroom with a scissors into 2 strips about 1 cm (⅜″) wide and 10 cm (4″) long (illus. 1). These will be the butterfly's antennae. Cut the other 3 mushrooms into 1 cm (⅜″) wide slices. Place one slice in the center, then arrange more slices on both sides, overlapping them to form a petal pattern (as in the *Flower Platter*, p. 21, illus. 2). Trim any uneven edges. Invert over the mashed potatoes (illus. 2) to form the butterfly's body.

❸ Pare the carrots. Cut the carrot and cucumber into thin 2×5 cm (¾″×2″) slices. Rub 1 teaspoon salt into the slices until pliable, then rinse off the salt. Marinate in ① 10 minutes. Drain.

❹ Heat the oil to about 300°F (149°C). Fry the vegetarian fish roe until fragrant and remove from the oil. Allow to cool. Cut the vegetarian fish roe, the vegetarian ham, and the vegetarian pork ribs into thin 2×5 cm (¾″×2″) slices.

❺ Arrange the ingredients in steps ❸ and ❹ the same as for the mushroom strips: arrange 2 petal patterns each with the vegetarian pork ribs, carrot, and cucumber; and one with the vegetarian fish roe and vegetarian ham. Place one each of the vegetarian pork rib petals and vegetarian ham petals to the left of the butterfly body, then place one cucumber petal and one carrot petal on that (illus. 3). This is the left wing of the butterfly. Arrange the 4 remaining petals in the same way to form the right wing. Finally, cut a maraschino cherry in half. Place the halves on the butterfly's "head", along with the peas, to form the eyes. Serve.

①蛋黃糕	egg yolk loaf	⑫香菇	black mushroom
②蛋白糕	egg white loaf	⑬青豆仁、香菇絲	peas, black mushroom strips
③素火腿	vegetarian ham	⑭紅辣椒	small red chili pepper
④小黃瓜片	gherkin cucumber slices	⑮紅蘿蔔	carrot
⑤櫻桃	maraschino cherry	⑯小黃瓜片	gherkin cucumber slices
⑥蛋黃糕	egg yolk loaf	⑰蛋白糕	egg white loaf
⑦紅蘿蔔	carrot	⑱素火腿	vegetarian ham
⑧素火腿	vegetarian ham	⑲蛋黃糕	egg yolk loaf
⑨蛋白糕	egg white loaf	⑳番茄片	tomato slices
⑩香菇絲	black mushroom	㉑大黃瓜片	cucumber slices
⑪馬鈴薯泥	mashed potatoes	㉒香菇	black mushroom

彩鳳拼盤

Phoenix Platter

材料：

素火腿·········	200公克		水··········	2大匙
紅蘿蔔片·········	80公克	①	太白粉·····	1½大匙
馬鈴薯泥·········	80公克		塩、味精·····	¼小匙
滷香菇(作法見花式拼盤)			水··········	2大匙
·············	4朵	②	太白粉·····	1½大匙
小黃瓜·········	1條		塩、味精·····	¼小匙
蛋·············	12個		糖··········	¾小匙
番茄(切片)·········	½個		醋··········	¾小匙
櫻桃·········	2個	③	麻油·········	¾小匙
青豆仁·········	1粒		胡椒粉·········	少許
大黃瓜片(5×3公分)	1片			
紅辣椒·········	1支			

❶ 取二個大碗將12個蛋的蛋黃及蛋白分開，其中12個蛋白加①料，12個蛋黃加②料拌勻，並分別倒入模型中，入蒸籠蒸15-20分鐘，即成蛋黃糕、蛋白糕，待涼後均取出。將1塊蛋黃糕，½塊的蛋白糕，200公克素火腿均切約0.3公分厚之半圓片，並將剩餘的½塊蛋白糕切絲備用。

❷ 滷香菇2朵切1公分寬之斜片，另2朵切成鳳爪狀(圖一)，櫻桃對切成4小塊。紅蘿蔔片以½小匙塩抓軟，並用水沖去塩份，再以③料醃10分鐘後瀝乾備用。

❸ 小黃瓜洗淨斜切片，大黃瓜片切佛手狀(圖二)備用。

❹ 將蛋黃糕片、蛋白糕片、素火腿片、小黃瓜片、香菇片各自重疊排列成鳳之右翼，另外再取蛋黃糕片、紅蘿蔔片、素火腿片、蛋白糕片、香菇片依右翼之排列方法排成鳳之左翼。

❺ 馬鈴薯泥捏成鳳上半身形狀，置於兩翼中央，蛋白糕絲排列覆蓋在馬鈴薯泥上，以青豆仁及香菇絲裝飾成鳳眼，紅辣椒之尾部裝飾成鳳嘴，再取一片紅蘿蔔切花，裝飾成鳳冠。

❻ 將剩餘之小黃瓜片3片及櫻桃片置鳳之尾端，再各以紅蘿蔔片、素火腿片、蛋黃糕片排列成長細彎形的鳳尾，其上端置番茄片及大黃瓜片，最後將香菇切成的鳳爪，裝飾在番茄片之左端即成。

INGREDIENTS:

200 g (7 oz.)		vegetarian ham
80 g (3 oz.)		carrot slices
80 g (3 oz.)		mashed potatoes
4		soy-seasoned Chinese black mushrooms (see *Flower Platter*, p. 21)
1		gherkin cucumber
12		eggs
½		tomato, sliced
2		maraschino cherries
1		pea
1 slice		cucumber (5×3 cm or 2″ ×1¼″)
1		small red chili pepper
①	2 T.	water
	1½ T.	cornstarch
	¼ t.	salt
②	2 T.	water
	1½ T.	cornstarch
	¼ t.	salt
③	¾ t.	sugar
	¾ t.	rice vinegar
	¾ t.	sesame oil
	pinch	pepper

❶ Separate the eggs, placing the yolks in one large bowl and the whites in another. Add ① to the bowl of egg whites and ② to the bowl of egg yolks. Mix each separately until well blended. Pour each into a small cake pan and steam 15 to 20 minutes. You now have an "egg yolk loaf" and "egg white loaf." Allow to cool then turn out of the cake pans. Cut the egg yolk loaf, half of the egg white loaf, and 200 g (7 oz.) vegetarian ham into 0.3 cm (⅛″) thick semicircular slices. Cut the remaining half of the egg white loaf into julienne strips.

❷ Cut 2 of the soy-seasoned black mushrooms into 1 cm (⅜″) thick diagonal slices. Cut the other two mushrooms into the shape of phoenix claws (illus. 1). Halve the maraschino cherries to make a total of 4 pieces. Rub ½ teaspoon salt into the carrot slices until pliable, then rinse off the salt. Marinate in ③ for 10 minutes. Drain.

❸ Wash the gherkin cucumbers and cut at an angle into slices. Fringe the cucumber slice ("Buddha's hand"; illus. 2). Set aside.

❹ Arrange the egg yolk loaf slices, egg white loaf slices, vegetarian ham slices, gherkin cucumber slices, and black mushroom slices to form the phoenix's right wing. Arrange more egg yolk loaf slices, carrot slices, vegetarian ham slices, egg white loaf slices and mushroom strips to form the left wing, similar to how you made the right wing.

❺ Make the phoenix's upper body from the mashed potatoes and place between the wings. Arrange the egg white loaf strips over the mashed potato body. Make the phoenix's eye from the pea and mushroom strips. Use the tip of a small red chili pepper for the beak. Carve the phoenix's comb from a slice of carrot.

❻ Make the end of the phoenix's tail from 3 of the remaining gherkin cucumber slices and the maraschino cherry halves. Then make a long, thin, curved tail from carrot slices, vegetarian ham slices, and egg yolk loaf slices. Top the upper portion with tomato slices and the fringed cucumber slice. Finally, place the mushroom claws to the left of the tomato slices. Serve.

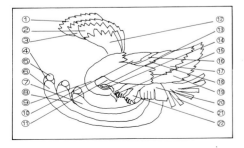

蘆筍紫捲

材料：

蘆筍	150公克	炸油	2杯
素烏魚子	50公克	沙拉醬	4大匙
生菜絲	50公克	① { 花生粉	1小匙
紫菜皮	3張	糖粉	1小匙

❶紫菜皮每張對切成2張共6小張，蘆筍川燙、漂涼、去老纖維，切與紫菜皮同長度，並分成6等分備用。

❷炸油燒7分熱（約300°F），將素烏魚子炸香，切成1公分寬長條並分成6等分備用。

❸將1份蘆筍、1份烏魚子、適量生菜絲及①料依次放在紫菜皮上，並將適量沙拉醬擠在上面（圖一），捲成圓筒狀（圖二），再切成4等份排盤即成。

Asparagus-Seaweed Rolls

INGREDIENTS:

150 g (⅓ lb.)	fresh asparagus
50 g (1¾ oz.)	vegetarian fish roe
50 g (1¾ oz.)	shredded lettuce
3 sheets	purple laver seaweed
2 c.	oil for frying
4 T.	mayonaise
① 1 t. each:	peanut powder, sugar

❶ Cut each sheet of purple laver in half to make a total of 6 sheets. Blanch the asparagus briefly in boiling water, cool in tap water, then peel. Cut into pieces the same length as the purple laver. Divide into 6 equal portions.

❷ Heat the oil to about 300°F (149°C). Deep-fry the vegetarian fish roe in the oil until fragrant. Cut into 1 cm (⅓″) slices. Divide into 6 equal portions.

❸ Place one portion of asparagus, one portion of vegetarian fish roe, some shredded lettuce, and some ① on each sheet of purple laver, and top with a bit of mayonaise (illus. 1). Roll into a cylindrical shape (illus. 2), cut into 4 equal pieces, and arrange on a serving platter. Serve.

6人份
SERVES 6

芝麻菠菜捲

材料：

菠菜⋯⋯⋯⋯⋯ 600公克		芝麻醬⋯⋯⋯ 1大匙
熟白芝麻⋯⋯⋯⋯ 1大匙	①	醬油膏⋯⋯⋯ 1小匙
		味精、糖⋯各½小匙

❶菠菜洗淨川燙，1分鐘後撈起，漂涼、瀝乾備用。
❷菠菜分成2等分，頭尾切齊(圖一)，分別以壽司捲
　捲緊(圖二)，再取出切3公分長段，擺在盤中，灑
　上熟芝麻、食時沾①料即成。

Sesame-Spinach Rolls

INGREDIENTS:

600 g (1⅓ lb.)		fresh spinach
1 T.		toasted white sesame seeds
	⎰1 T.	sesame paste
①	⎨1 t.	thick soy sauce
	⎱½ t.	sugar

❶ Wash the spinach thoroughly and blanch in boiling water for 1 minute. Cool in tap water and drain well.
❷ Divide the spinach into 2 equal portions. Cut off the ends so each bunch is the same length (illus. 1). Roll each portion of spinach tightly into a cylinder with a bamboo *sushi* mat (*sudare*; illus. 2), then cut into 3 cm (1¼") lengths. Arrange on a serving platter and sprinkle on the toasted sesame seeds. Dip in ① before eating.

6人份
SERVES 6

拌素蜇皮

Vegetarian Jellyfish Salad

材料：

白蘿蔔…………	350公克		紅辣椒絲……	20公克
素魷魚…………	180公克		薑絲…………	20公克
小黃瓜…………	150公克	①	麻油…………	2小匙
塩…………………	1小匙		塩、味精……	½小匙
			糖、胡椒粉…各少許	

❶白蘿蔔去皮與小黃瓜均切５公分長細絲（圖一），入
　１小匙塩醃約10分鐘，再以冷開水沖去塩份備用。

❷素魷魚切絲（圖二），川燙後再以冷開水漂涼；最後
　與白蘿蔔絲，小黃瓜絲及①料拌勻即成。

INGREDIENTS:

350 g (¾ lb.)	Chinese white radish
180 g (6 oz.)	vegetarian squid
150 g (⅓ lb.)	gherkin cucumbers
1 t.	salt

	20 g (¾ oz.) each:	small red chili pepper shreds, ginger root shreds
①	2 t.	sesame oil
	½ t.	salt
	pinch each:	sugar, pepper

❶ Peel the Chinese white radish. Cut the white radish and the gherkin cucumbers into 5 cm (2″) julienne strips (illus. 1). Add 1 teaspoon salt and set aside for 10 minutes. Wash off the salt with cold water.

❷ Cut the vegetarian squid into julienne strips (illus. 2). Blanch briefly in boiling water, then cool in a bowl of cold water. Toss with the white radish and gherkin cucumber strips and ①. Serve.

6人份

SERVES 6

油辣西芹

Spicy Marinated Celery

材料：

西芹············ 600公克		麻油············ 1小匙
紅辣椒絲··········20公克	①	塩、味精···各½小匙
		辣油··········½小匙

❶西芹洗淨川燙３分鐘，取出沖冷開水瀝乾水份備用。

❷將燙好的西芹去老纖維（圖一），切５公分長段（圖二），再與①料及紅辣椒絲拌勻即成。

INGREDIENTS:

600 g (1⅓ lb.)		celery
20 g (¾ oz.)		small red chili pepper shreds
①	1 t.	sesame oil
	½ t.	salt
	½ t.	chili oil

❶ Wash the celery thoroughly. Blanch in boiling water 3 minutes, then cool in cold water. Drain well.

❷ Remove the tough strings from the celery (illus. 1) and cut into 5 cm (2″) long pieces (illus. 2). Toss well with ① and the red chili shreds. Serve.

6人份
SERVES 6

苦瓜麵腸

材料：

苦瓜	300公克		醬油	1大匙
麵腸	270公克	①	味精	少許
豆豉末	1大匙		胡椒粉	少許
紅椒末	2小匙	②	醬油、麻油 各1大匙	
九層塔末	2小匙		味精	½小匙
炸油	4杯		水或素高湯	¾杯
		③	水	1大匙
			太白粉	⅔小匙

❶ 苦瓜去籽洗淨，與麵腸均切2×5公分長條狀（圖一）。苦瓜入鍋川燙撈起，麵腸入①料醃約15分鐘備用。

❷ 炸油燒7分熱（約300°F），將麵腸過油撈起與苦瓜先後排入扣碗中（圖二）。

❸ 鍋內留油1大匙，爆香豆豉及紅椒末，拌入②料燒開，隨即倒出，放在排好之苦瓜麵腸上，入蒸籠蒸15分鐘，取出倒出湯汁，其他材料倒扣盤中備用。

❹ 餘汁與水入鍋燒開，以③料勾芡淋在苦瓜麵腸上，並灑上九層塔末即成。

Bitter Melon with Vegetarian Sausage

INGREDIENTS:

	300 g (⅔ lb.)	bitter melon (balsam pear; foo gwa)
	270 g (9½ oz.)	vegetarian (wheat gluten) sausage
	1 T.	Chinese fermented black beans
	2 t. each:	minced red chili pepper, minced fresh basil leaves
	4. c.	oil for deep frying
①	1 T.	soy sauce
	pinch	pepper
②	1 T. each:	soy sauce, sesame oil
	¾ c.	water or vegetarian stock
③	1 T.	water
	⅔ t.	cornstarch

❶ Remove the seeds from the bitter melon and wash. Cut the bitter melon and vegetarian sausage into 2×5 cm (¾″×2″) strips (illus. 1). Blanch the bitter melon briefly in boiling water and remove. Add ① to the vegetarian sausage and allow to marinate about 15 minutes.

❷ Heat the oil to about 300°F (149°C). Immerse the vegetarian sausage briefly in the hot oil and remove. Arrange in a bowl together with the bitter melon (illus. 2).

❸ Leave 1 tablespoon oil in the wok or frying pan, and fry the fermented black beans and minced red chili until fragrant. Add ② and bring to a boil. Pour over the top of the bitter melon and vegetarian sausage. Place in a steamer and steam 15 minutes. Remove from the steamer and pour the liquid into a container. Invert the bowl to transfer the ingredients to a plate.

❹ Bring the poured-off liquid and the water to a boil in the wok, thicken with ③, then pour over the bitter melon and vegetarian sausage. Sprinkle the minced basil leaves over the top and serve.

6人份
SERVES 6

奶油連白捲

材料：

高麗菜葉	6片		麻油	1小匙
小黃瓜絲	100公克	①	塩、味精	³⁄₈小匙
紅蘿蔔絲	80公克		胡椒粉	少許
鮮香菇絲	40公克		鮮奶、水	各½杯
白豆支	10公克	②	太白粉	1小匙
薑末、芹菜末	各⅔大匙		塩、味精	各¼小匙
植物油	2大匙			

❶高麗菜洗淨、川燙、漂冷、瀝乾，並去葉梗（圖一）
；白豆支以水泡軟瀝乾均備用。

❷鍋熱入油，爆香薑末，續入白豆支、紅蘿蔔絲、小
黃瓜絲及香菇絲拌炒數下，再入①料及芹菜末拌勻
，盛起去湯汁，分成6等分的餡。

❸1片高麗菜葉包入1份餡，捲成6公分長圓筒狀（
圖二），共包6條，入蒸籠以大火蒸10分鐘，取出斜
對切排盤。

❹②料拌勻，入鍋煮沸淋在高麗菜捲上即成。

6人份
SERVES 6

Creamed Cabbage Rolls

INGREDIENTS:

6	cabbage leaves
100 g (3½ oz.)	shredded gherkin cucumber
80 g (3 oz.)	shredded carrot
40 g (1½ oz.)	shredded fresh Chinese black mushroom (*shiitake*)
10 g (⅓ oz.)	dried pressed bean curd strips
⅔ T. each:	minced ginger root, minced Chinese celery
2 T.	vegetable oil
① ⎰ 1 t.	sesame oil
⎱ ³⁄₈ t.	salt
⎰ pinch	pepper
② ⎰ ½ c. each:	fresh milk, water
⎰ 1 t.	cornstarch
⎱ ¼ t.	salt

❶ Wash the cabbage, blanch briefly in boiling water, and cool in a bowl of tap water. Drain and cut off the tough stems (illus. 1). Soak the dried pressed bean curd strips in water until soft, and drain.

❷ Heat a wok or frying pan, add the vegetable oil, and fry the minced ginger briefly. Add the dried pressed bean curd strips, shredded carrot, shredded gherkin cucumber, and shredded mushroom, and stir-fry. Next add ① and the minced Chinese celery, mixing well. Remove to a container, drain off the liquid, and divide into 6 equal portions. This is the filling.

❸ Roll one portion of filling inside each cabbage leaf to form a 6 cm (2½") cylinder shape (illus. 2). Place the six cabbage rolls in a steamer and steam 10 minutes over high heat. Remove, cut at an angle into pieces, and arrange on a serving plate.

❹ Mix ② until well blended and bring to a boil. Pour over the cabbage rolls, and serve.

元寶珍排

Stuffed Mushrooms with Shark Fins

材料：

香菇·····················18朵		
綠竹筍(淨重)··· 300公克	① {	太白粉········ 3大匙
素海蔘·············70公克		塩、味精······½小匙
花菜·················70公克		糖·········· ½小匙
紅蘿蔔·············30公克		水或素高湯··· 3大匙
荸薺末 ⎫		醬油·········· 2小匙
紅蘿蔔末 ⎬ ·····各50公克	② {	麻油·········· 2小匙
玉米筍末 ⎪		塩、味精······¼小匙
毛豆末 ⎭		糖·········· ¼小匙
芹菜末·············· 1大匙		水或素高湯··· 1½杯
炸油················· 4杯	③ {	麻油·········· 1小匙
		塩、味精···各¼小匙
		胡椒粉··········少許
	④ {	水··········· 1大匙
		太白粉········ 1小匙

❶香菇均泡軟去蒂，選出12朵大小相同且圓者備用。

❷紅蘿蔔末、荸薺末、玉米筍末、毛豆末與①料拌勻分成12等份的餡，再將每份餡分別鑲入每朵香菇內（圖一），成12個元寶；再將元寶入蒸籠（圖二），以大火蒸10分鐘，取出排成一圓圈備用。

❸竹筍去老纖維，切2×3公分片狀，再切成佛手狀（同一品排翅的切法），紅蘿蔔去皮與素海蔘均切與竹筍同大小之片狀，花菜洗淨修去老纖維，均備用。

❹炸油燒8分熱（350°F），將竹筍炸乾水份，略呈金黃色時（圖三）撈起瀝油。

❺鍋內留油1大匙，先將剩餘的6朵香菇、紅蘿蔔片爆香，再入花椰菜、竹筍片及素海蔘一起拌炒數下，續入②料，以文火燜煮5分鐘，待汁略乾即盛入盤中。

❻將③料煮沸，以④料勾芡淋在元寶上即成。

INGREDIENTS:

18	dried Chinese black mushrooms
300 g (⅔ lb.)	fresh bamboo shoots (net wt.)
70 g (2½ oz.)	vegetarian sea cucumber
70 g (2½ oz.)	cauliflower
30 g (1 oz.)	carrot
50 g (1¾ oz.) each:	minced water chestnuts, minced carrot, minced baby corn, minced fresh soybeans
1 T.	minced Chinese celery
4 c.	oil for deep frying
① 3 T.	cornstarch
½ t. each:	salt, sugar
② 3 T.	water or vegetarian stock
2 t. each:	soy sauce, sesame oil
¼ t. each:	salt, sugar
③ 1½ c.	water or vegetarian stock
1 t.	sesame oil
¼ t.	salt
pinch	pepper
④ 1 T.	water
1 t.	cornstarch

❶ Soak the dried mushrooms until soft and remove the stems. Choose the 12 mushrooms that are the roundest and closest in size.

❷ Mix the minced carrot, minced water chestnuts, minced baby corn, and minced fresh soybeans with ① until well combined. Divide into 12 equal portions. Press one portion of this filling into each mushroom (illus. 1). Place the stuffed mushrooms in a steamer (illus. 2) and steam 10 minutes over high heat. Remove and arrange in a circle.

❸ Trim off the tough, fibrous portions of the bamboo shoots and cut into 2×3 cm (¾″×1¼″) slices. Slash on one edge to fringe ("Buddha's hand", the same as for Vegetarian Shark Fins). Pare the carrot. Cut the carrot and the vegetarian sea cucumber into the same size slices as the bamboo shoots. Wash the cauliflower and cut off the tough, fibrous portions.

❹ Heat the oil to about 350°F (177°C) and deep-fry the bamboo shoots until most of the moisture has evaporated and they are golden brown (illus. 3). Remove from the oil and drain.

❺ Pour off all but 1 tablespoon of the oil from the wok. Fry the remaining 6 mushrooms and the carrot slices briefly, then add the cauliflower, bamboo shoots, and vegetarian sea cucumber. Stir-fry briefly, then add ② and braise over low heat 5 minutes, until the sauce is reduced. Transfer to a serving plate.

❻ Bring ③ to a boil, thicken with ④, and pour over the stuffed mushrooms. Serve.

如意豆腐

As-You-Wish Bean Curd Rolls

材料：

芥菜	300公克		
紅蘿蔔絲	80公克	② 蛋	2個
小黃瓜絲	80公克	太白粉	2小匙
紫菜皮	2張	水	1杯
嫩豆腐	1½塊	麻油	1小匙
植物油	2大匙	③ 塩	少許
① 薑汁	1大匙	味精	少許
麻油	½大匙	胡椒粉	少許
味精	½小匙	④ 水	1大匙
塩	⅜小匙	太白粉	⅔小匙
胡椒粉	少許		

❶芥菜切劍形（圖一），入鍋川燙、漂冷，豆腐攪成泥與①料拌勻均備用。

❷②料拌勻分成2等份，鍋熱入油，以小火將每份蛋糊煎成直徑約15公分的蛋皮備用。

❸豆腐泥抹在蛋皮上（圖二），上放1張紫菜皮，再抹1層豆腐泥，最後放紅蘿蔔絲及小黃瓜絲，將整個餡包捲起來成直徑約4公分的圓筒狀（圖三），另一份也以同樣作法處理好，同入蒸籠以大火蒸10分鐘，取出待涼切0.5公分寬斜片，排入扣碗中，再蒸1分鐘，即取出倒扣盤中，並以芥菜圍邊備用。

❹③料煮沸，以④料勾芡淋在如意豆腐上即成。

INGREDIENTS:

300 g (⅔ lb.)		fresh mustard greens
80 g (3 oz.) each:		shredded carrot, shredded gherkin cucumber
2 sheets		purple laver seaweed
1½ cakes		soft bean curd
2 T.		vegetable oil
①	1 T.	ginger root juice
	½ T.	sesame oil
	⅜ t.	salt
	pinch	pepper
②	2	eggs
	2 t.	cornstarch
③	1 c.	water
	1 t.	sesame oil
	pinch each:	salt, pepper
④	1 T.	water
	⅔ t.	cornstarch

❶ Cut the mustard greens as illustrated (illus. 1) and blanch briefly in boiling water. Cool in a bowl of tap water. Mash the bean curd and mix in ① until thoroughly combined.

❷ Mix ② thoroughly and divide into 2 equal portions. Heat a wok and add the oil. Fry each portion of the egg mixture over low heat into an omelette 15 cm (6″) in diameter.

❸ Spread some mashed bean curd on an omelette (illus. 2), place a sheet of purple laver on the mashed bean curd, then spread another layer of mashed bean curd on the seaweed. Finally, top with shredded carrot and shredded gherkin cucumber, and roll into a cylindrical shape about 4 cm (1½″) in diameter (illus. 3). Follow the same procedure for the other omelette. Place in a steamer and steam 10 minutes over high heat. Remove, allow to cool, and cut into 0.5 cm (¼″) thick diagonal slices. Arrange in a bowl and steam 1 minute. Invert onto a plate, and arrange the mustard greens around the edge.

❹ Bring ③ to a boil, thicken with ④, and pour over the As-You-Wish Bean Curd Rolls. Serve.

盤若蜜

Vegetarian Honey Ham

材料：

圓形素火腿……	150公克
黑棗…………	120公克
白土司…………	6片

① { 蜂蜜………… 3大匙
糖或碎冰糖… 2大匙
桂花醬……… 1小匙 }

② { 水……………… ½杯
櫻桃汁……… 1大匙
糖………… 1小匙 }

③ { 水……………… ½大匙
太白粉……… ½小匙
桂花醬……… 1小匙 }

❶素火腿切0.2公分厚半圓薄片，排入扣碗中(圖一)，依序入黑棗(圖二)及①料，再入蒸籠以大火蒸20分鐘，取出倒扣盤中，餘汁留用。

❷餘汁與②料入鍋煮沸，以③料勾芡，加入桂花醬淋在火腿上，食時以土司夾食即成。

■土司去邊，對切成兩片，每小片再片開，不必切斷，入蒸籠以大火蒸1分鐘，口感更佳。

INGREDIENTS:

150 g (⅓ lb.)	round vegetarian (bean curd) ham
120 g (4 oz.)	prunes
6 slices	white bread

① { 3 T. — honey
2 T. — sugar or crushed rock candy
1 t. — osmanthus jam }

② { ½ C. — water
1 T. — maraschino cherry juice
1 t. — sugar }

③ { ½ T. — water
½ t. — cornstarch
1 t. — osmanthus jam }

❶ Cut the vegetarian ham into 0.2 cm (1/16″) thick semicircles and arrange in a bowl (illus. 1). On this place , in order, the prunes (illus. 2) and ①. Place in a steamer and steam 20 minutes over high heat. Remove from the steamer and invert onto a plate. Reserve the liquid.

❷ Add the reserved liquid and ② to a wok and bring to a boil. Thicken with ③ and add the osmanthus jam. Pour over the vegetarian ham. Place some vegetarian ham inside a piece of white bread, like a sandwich, to eat.

■ Cut the crusts off the white bread, cut each slice in half, then split open each piece like a hot dog bun. Steam about 1 minute over high heat before serving for even tastier results.

6人份
SERVES 6

珍珠綉球

Pearl Balls

材料：

糯米·····················½杯	② ｛ 塩、味精···各¼小匙
豆苗·················· 120公克	水················· 1杯
麵輪·················40公克	麻油············ 1小匙
荸薺·················35公克	③ ｛ 塩、味精······¼小匙
香菇·················10公克	糖············¼小匙
油··················· 1大匙	胡椒粉··········少許
① ｛ 太白粉········ 3大匙	④ ｛ 水·············· 1大匙
塩、味精·····½小匙	太白粉········⅔小匙
糖············½小匙	
麻油、胡椒粉···少許	

❶糯米洗淨加水泡１小時，取出瀝乾，豆苗去老莖洗淨。

❷麵輪泡軟擠乾水份，香菇泡軟去蒂，荸薺洗淨，將以上材料均切末與①料拌成餡，分成12等份備用。

❸將每份餡捏成魚丸狀(圖一)，滾上糯米(圖二)，入蒸籠以大火蒸20分鐘，取出是爲珍珠綉球。

❹鍋熱入油１大匙，炒熟豆苗，入②料拌勻盛起排盤，將珍珠綉球置豆苗上，將③料煮沸，以④料勾芡淋在珍珠綉球上即成。

■此道菜之餡，可加入少許當歸末，味道更佳。

6人份
SERVES 6

INGREDIENTS:

	½ c.	glutinous rice
	120 g (¼ lb.)	peavine (or other) greens
	40 g (1½ oz.)	dried wheat gluten wheels
	35 g (1 oz.)	water chestnuts
	10 g (⅓-½ oz.)	dried Chinese black mushrooms
	1 T.	vegetable oil
①	3 T.	cornstarch
	½ t. each:	salt, sugar,
	dash each:	sesame oil, pepper
②	¼ t.	salt
③	1 c.	water
	1 t.	sesame oil
	¼ t. each:	salt, sugar
	pinch	pepper
④	1 T.	water
	⅔ t.	cornstarch

❶ Wash the glutinous rice and soak in water for 1 hour. Drain. Remove the tough portions of the peavine greens and wash.

❷ Soak the dried wheat gluten wheels until soft. Squeeze out the excess moisture. Soak the mushrooms until soft and remove the stems. Wash the water chestnuts. Mince the above ingredients and mix with ① to make the filling. Divide into 12 equal portions.

❸ Roll each portion of filling into a firm ball (illus. 1). Roll in the glutinous rice (illus. 2). Place in a steamer and steam 20 minutes over high heat. Remove to a plate.

❹ Heat a wok and add 1 tablespoon oil. Stir-fry the peavine greens until just done. Stir in ② until well combined. Transfer to a serving plate. Place the pearl balls on top of the greens. Bring ③ to a boil, thicken with ④, then pour over the pearl balls. Serve.

■ A little Chinese angelica (*tang kuei*) may be added to the filling for extra flavor.

荷花豆腐

Lotus Blossom Bean Curd

材料：

豆腐	1塊
蛋白	2個
青江菜	2棵
髮菜	少許
白果	12顆
毛豆	10顆
湯匙	12支
醬油碟子	1個

① 蛋白 …… 1個
薑汁、麻油各 1小匙
味精、塩 …… 各½小匙
胡椒粉 …… ½小匙

② 水或素高湯 …… 1½杯
麻油 …… 1小匙
塩、味精 …… ½小匙
胡椒粉 …… ½小匙

③ 水 …… 1大匙
太白粉 …… 1小匙

❶ 青江菜剝成片狀去葉，只留5公分長段，再切細絲，髮菜泡軟備用，豆腐與①料拌成泥(圖一)，蛋白打至發泡備用。

❷ 將豆腐泥倒入醬油碟子及12支湯匙內，上抹蛋白，依序將毛豆、白果、青江菜絲、髮菜裝飾在蛋白上(圖二)，入蒸籠以中火蒸10分鐘，即將豆腐泥自器皿中取出排盤。

❸ ②料燒開，以③料勾芡，淋在豆腐上即成。

INGREDIENTS:

1 cake	bean curd
2	egg whites
2 bunches	*ching kang tsai* (or other leafy greens)
small bunch	hair seaweed (*fa tsai*)
12	gingko nuts
10	fresh soybeans
12	Chinese style soup spoons
1	small soy sauce dish

① 1 — egg white
1 t. each: ginger root juice, sesame oil
½ t. each: salt, pepper

② 1½ c. water or vegetarian stock
1 t. sesame oil
½ t. each: salt, pepper

③ 1 T. water
1 t. cornstarch

❶ Break off each stalk from the *ching kang tsai*, then cut off the leafy portion, leaving 5 cm (2″) of the stalk. Cut the stalks into julienne strips. Soak the hair seaweed until soft. Set aside. Mash the bean curd together with ① (illus. 1). Beat the 2 egg whites until foamy.

❷ Fill the soy sauce dish and 12 Chinese style soup spoons with the mashed bean curd mixture. Brush (or rub on with a finger) a little egg white over each. Next arrange the fresh soybeans, gingko nuts, shredded greens, and hair seaweed on the top of each in a decorative pattern (illus. 2). Steam 10 minutes over medium heat. Remove the steamed mixture from the spoons and dish and arrange on a serving plate.

❸ Bring ② to a boil, thicken with ③, and pour over the bean curd. Serve.

6人份
SERVES 6

香脆魚片

Fried Fish Canapés

材料：

素烏魚子········· 100公克	麵粉············· ½杯
白土司·············· 3片	冰水············· ¼杯
紅蘿蔔末··········· 1大匙	沙拉油········· ½大匙
巴西利末··········· 1大匙 ①	塩、味精······ ¼小匙
黑芝麻············· 1大匙	胡椒粉··········· 少許
炸油·············· 6杯	蛋············· ½個

❶①料調成麵糊，土司去邊，每片對切成4小片，烏魚子切0.5×4×4公分片狀備用。

❷每片土司上放1片烏魚子，再塗1層麵糊 (圖一)，最上面以黑芝麻、紅蘿蔔末、巴西利末點綴 (圖二)。

❸炸油燒6分熱 (約250°F)，將❷炸成金黃色撈起瀝油即成。

INGREDIENTS:

100 g (3½ oz.)	vegetarian fish roe
3 slices	white bread
1 T. each:	minced carrot, minced parsley, black sesame seeds
6 c.	oil for frying
½ c.	flour
¼ c.	ice water
① ½ T.	oil
¼ t.	salt
pinch	pepper
½	egg

❶ Mix the ingredients in ① to form a smooth batter. Trim the crusts off the bread and cut each slice into 4 small squares. Cut the vegetarian fish roe into 0.5×4×4 cm (¼″ × 1½″ × 1½″) slices.

❷ Place one slice of vegetarian fish roe on each square of bread, then spread on some batter (illus. 1). Garnish the top with the black sesame seeds, minced carrot, and minced parsley (illus. 2).

❸ Heat the oil for frying to about 250°F (121°C). Fry the bread as prepared in step ❷ until golden. Drain off the excess oil and serve.

6人份
SERVES 6

金玉滿堂 / Vegetarian Snack Platter

材料：

紅豆沙………… 180公克		炸油…………… 6杯	
芋頭(淨重)…… 150公克		①	麵粉………… 1杯
滷好之豆包（同第19頁滷			水………… ⅓杯
香菇作法）………… 2個			塩、味精…… ¼小匙
紫菜皮………… 2張			蛋………… 1個
金菇(淨重)……60公克		②	糖………… 3大匙
高麗菜絲………60公克			太白粉……… 2大匙
豆皮…………… 1½張		③	塩、味精……各少許
藕粉…………… 1½杯			
白芝麻…………… ½杯			

❶ ①料拌勻成麵糊備用。

❷ 紅豆沙分成6等份，分別搓圓後沾水滾藕粉（圖一），入開水中煮，待浮出水面即撈起，再滾藕粉，再入開水中煮，如此反覆三次，成藕球備用。

❸ 芋頭切片蒸熟，入②料拌成泥，分6等份，各搓成圓球後，沾水滾上白芝麻成芝麻芋球備用。

❹ 豆包2個切成6等份，紫菜皮2張等切為6小張，將每份豆包以1小張的紫菜皮包捲成約6公分長之條狀（圖二），接口以麵糊黏緊，共做6條備用。

❺ 鍋熱入油1大匙，將高麗菜絲及金菇炒熟入③料拌勻，取出倒去湯汁，分成6等份餡備用。

❻ 豆皮1張半等切成6小張，將每份餡以1小張豆皮包捲成6公分之長條狀，接口以麵糊黏緊成小鷄腿，共包成6隻小鷄腿備用。

❼ 炸油燒7分熱(300°F)，將藕球及芝麻球分別入鍋炸至金黃色，撈起瀝油排盤，再將❹料左右兩面沾麵糊（圖三），入鍋炸至金黃色，撈起瀝油排盤，最後將小鷄腿整隻沾麵糊，入鍋炸至金黃色，撈起瀝油排盤即成。

Vegetarian Snack Platter

INGREDIENTS:

180 g (6 oz.)		sweet red bean (adzuki) paste
150 g (⅓ lb.)		taro root (net weight)
2		soy-seasoned bean curd pockets (season according to the method for making soy-seasoned mushrooms in *Flower Platter*, p. 21, step 1).
2 sheets		purple laver seaweed
60 g (2 oz.)		enoki (golden mushrooms; net weight)
60 g (2 oz.)		shredded cabbage
1½ squares		bean curd skin
1½ c.		lotus root powder
½ c.		white sesame seeds
6 c.		oil for frying
①	1 c.	flour
	⅓ c.	water
	¼ t.	salt
	1	egg
②	3 T.	sugar
	2 T.	cornstarch
③	pinch	salt

❶ Mix ① into a smooth batter.

❷ Divide the red bean paste into 6 equal portions and roll each into a ball. Dip each separately in water, then roll in the lotus root powder (illus. 1). Place in a pot of boiling water. Allow to boil until the balls rise to the surface, then remove. Roll in the lotus root powder again, and return to the pot of boiling water. Repeat this same procedure three times.

❸ Cut the taro root into slices and steam until soft. Mash together with ②. Divide into 6 equal portions and roll into balls. Dip in water, then roll in the white sesame seeds.

❹ Cut the 2 bean curd pockets into a total of 6 equal portions, and the 2 sheets of purple laver seaweed into a total of 6 small squares. Wrap each of the pieces of bean curd pocket in a small seaweed square forming a 6 cm (2½") long cylinder shape (illus. 1). Seal the opening tightly with batter.

❺ Heat a wok or frying pan and add 1 tablespoon oil. Stir-fry the shredded cabbage and the enoki until barely done, then mix in ③ until well blended. Remove from the wok, pour off the liquid, and divide into 6 equal portions of filling. Set aside.

❻ Cut the 1½ squares bean curd skin into a total of 6 equally-sized portions. Wrap one portion of the vegetable filling in each of the 6 pieces of bean curd skin, forming a cylinder shape. Seal the opening tightly with batter. These are "vegetarian chicken legs."

❼ Heat the oil for frying to about 300°F (149°C). Deep-fry until golden first the lotus root powder balls, then the sesame balls. Drain off the excess oil, then arrange on a serving platter. Next dip both sides of the seaweed rolls prepared in step ❹ in the batter (illus. 3) and deep-fry until golden. Drain off the excess oil and arrange on the serving platter. Finally, dip the vegetarian chicken legs into the batter and deep-fry until golden. Drain off the excess oil and arrange on the serving platter. Serve.

烤素方

Vegetable Mille-Feuille

材料：

紅蘿蔔末	100公克	炸油	6杯
竹筍末	100公克	① 麵粉	1杯
香菇	10公克	水	½杯
豆皮	4張	油	1大匙
芹菜末	1大匙	塩、味精	¼小匙
熟芹菜段	12段	蛋	1個
白土司麵包	6片		

❶①料拌勻調成麵糊備用。

❷香菇泡軟去蒂切細末，與紅蘿蔔末、筍末、芹菜末拌勻成餡，均分3等份備用。

❸豆皮4張，每張均修飾成約30×20公分的長方形，豆皮1張抹上1層麵糊，再將1份餡均勻地灑在麵糊上（圖一），再取1張豆皮覆蓋其上（圖二），第2張豆皮上再抹1層麵糊，上灑第2份餡，如此共反覆3次，共有3層餡，4層皮，是爲素大方。

❹炸油燒6分熱（約250°F），將素大方整個沾麵糊（圖三），入鍋油炸，並在其表面以牙籤穿洞以透氣，再改小火，待兩面均炸成金黃色後，開大火炸酥撈起瀝油，切12小片排盤即成。

❺食時沾甜麵醬並以土司麵包及熟芹菜段夾食即可。

■土司麵包去邊對切成2半，入蒸籠以大火蒸1分鐘，熟芹菜段則視個人口味添加即可。

INGREDIENTS:

	100 g (3½ oz.)	minced carrot
	100 g (3½ oz.)	minced bamboo shoots
	10 g (⅓ oz.)	dried Chinese black mushrooms
	4 sheets	bean curd skin
	1 T.	minced Chinese celery
	12 pieces	cooked Chinese celery
	6 slices	white bread
	6 c.	oil for frying
①	1 c.	flour
	½ c.	water
	1 T.	oil
	¼ t.	salt
	1	egg

❶ Mix ① into a smooth batter and set aside.

❷ Soak the dried mushrooms until soft, cut off and discard the stems, and mince finely. Mix with the minced carrot, bamboo shoots, and celery to form a filling. Divide into 3 equal portions.

❸ Trim each of the 4 squares of bean curd skin into a rectangle about 30×20 cm (12″×8″). Spread a layer of batter on one of the sheets of bean curd skin, then sprinkle one portion of filling over that (illus. 1). Top with a second sheet of bean curd skin (illus. 2). Spread a layer of batter on the top of this second sheet, then sprinkle the second portion of filling on it. Repeat this step with the third sheet of bean curd skin and third portion of filling. Top with the fourth sheet of bean curd skin. This is the "vegetable mille-feuille."

❹ Heat the oil for frying to about 250°F (121°C). Dip the whole vegetable mille-feuille into the batter (illus. 3) and ease into the oil to deep-fry. Prick holes in it with a fork to allow the hot steam and air to escape. Lower the heat. Turn the heat back up to high after both sides have been fried golden brown. Continue to deep-fry briefly until crisp, then remove from the oil and drain. Cut into 12 small pieces. Arrange on a serving platter and serve.

❺ To eat, dip first in sweet bean paste, then place inside a piece of white bread with some cooked celery. Eat as a sandwich.

■ Trim the crusts off each slice of white bread, cut in half, and steam 1 minute before serving. The cooked celery may be added according to individual taste.

南國香捲

Banana-Chicken Rolls

材料：

香蕉	200公克	麵粉		1杯
素鷄	60公克	水		½杯
豆皮	2張	玉米粉		2大匙
炸油	6杯 ①	沙拉油		1大匙
		塩、味精		½小匙
		胡椒粉		少許
		蛋		1個

❶①料調成麵糊備用，香蕉去皮與素鷄均切5×1.5公分條狀備用。

❷豆腐皮每張切6小張，共12張。將香蕉、素鷄各一條放在豆皮上（圖一），捲成筒狀（圖二），接口以麵糊粘緊是爲香捲備用。

❸炸油燒7分熱（約300°Ｆ），將香捲沾上麵糊，入鍋炸成金黃色，撈起瀝油排盤，食時沾番茄醬即成。

INGREDIENTS:

200 g (7 oz.)	bananas
60 g (2 oz.)	vegetarian chicken
2 sheets	bean curd skin
6 c.	oil for frying
1 c.	flour
½ c.	water
2 T.	cornstarch
① 1 T.	vegetable oil
½ t.	salt
pinch	pepper
1	egg

❶ Mix ① into a smooth batter and set aside. Peel the bananas. Cut the bananas and the vegetarian chicken into 5×1.5 cm (2″×⅝″) strips.

❷ Cut each sheet of bean curd skin into 6 small squares, making a total of 12. Place one strip each of banana and vegetarian chicken inside each small square of bean curd skin (illus. 1) and roll into a cylinder shape (illus. 2). Seal the opening tightly with batter. Repeat until you have 12 rolls.

❸ Heat the oil to about 300°F (149°C). Dip each roll in the batter and deep-fry until golden. Remove from the oil, drain, and arrange on a serving platter. The rolls may be dipped in ketchup before eating.

6人份
SERVES 6

香酥豬排

Vegetarian Cutlet

材料：

香菇蒂············ 300公克	麻油、酒···各 1大匙
芹菜末·············· 1大匙	薑汁··········· 1大匙
炸油··················· 6杯	玉米粉········ 1大匙
①	塩、味精···各 1小匙
	糖·············½小匙
	胡椒粉··········少許
	蛋················· 3個

❶香菇蒂泡軟去硬頭，以打肉器壓碎（圖一）入芹菜末
　及①料拌勻醃 5 分鐘後，分成四等份，將每份壓成
　1 公分厚豬排狀（圖二），入蒸籠大火蒸15分鐘，取
　出是為素排。
❷炸油燒熱，將素排入油鍋炸成金黃色，取出切 1 公
　分寬片即成。

INGREDIENTS:

300 g (⅔ lb.)	dried Chinese black mushroom stems
1 T.	minced Chinese celery
6 c.	oil for frying
① 1 T. each:	sesame oil, rice wine, ginger juice, cornstarch
1 t.	salt
½ t.	sugar
pinch	pepper
3	eggs

❶ Soak the mushroom stems until soft and
remove the tough ends. Pound with a meat
mallet until well chopped (illus. 1). Stir in the
minced celery and ① until combined. Allow
to marinate 5 minutes, then divide into 4
equal portions. Form each portion into a 1 cm
(⅜″) thick patty resembling a pork cutlet (illus.
2). Steam 15 minutes over high heat.
❷ Heat the oil and deep-fry the cutlets until
golden. Remove from the oil, cut into 1 cm
(⅜″) wide slices, and serve.

6 人份
SERVES 6

美味素鵝

材料：

金菇‥‥‥‥‥‥ 120公克	水‥‥‥‥‥‥‥ 1杯
香菇‥‥‥‥‥‥25公克	薑末‥‥‥‥‥‥ 1大匙
豆皮‥‥‥‥‥‥‥10張	芹菜末‥‥‥‥‥ 1大匙
炸油‥‥‥‥‥‥‥ 6杯	香菜末‥‥‥‥‥ 1大匙

① { 醬油‥‥‥‥ 1小匙
味精、糖‥‥各少許
胡椒粉‥‥‥‥少許 }

② { 九層塔末‥‥‥ 1大匙
醬油‥‥‥‥‥ 1小匙
麻油‥‥‥‥‥ 1小匙
塩、味精‥‥‥‥少許
糖、胡椒粉‥‥‥少許 }

❶ 香菇泡軟去蒂切絲，與金菇洗淨去頭，以油2大匙
炒熟，並入①料拌勻成餡。

❷ ②料入鍋煮開，過濾成滷汁備用。

❸ 每張豆皮刷上滷汁（圖一），重疊放一起共10層，最
上層中央放餡，再捲成15×5公分之長筒狀（圖二），
入蒸籠以大火蒸5分鐘取出待涼，即為素鵝。

❹ 剩餘之炸油燒熱，將素鵝入油鍋炸成金黃色，撈起
瀝油再切2公分寬片排盤即成。

Vegetarian Goose

INGREDIENTS:

120 g (4 oz.)	enoki (golden mushrooms)
25 g (1 oz.)	dried Chinese black mushrooms
10 sheets	bean curd skin
6 c.	oil for frying

① { 1 t.
pinch each:
1 c. }
soy sauce
sugar, pepper
water

② { 1 T. each:

1 t. each:
pinch each: }
minced ginger root, minced Chinese
celery, minced fresh coriander
(Chinese parsley), minced fresh basil
leaves
soy sauce, sesame oil
salt, sugar, pepper

❶ Soak the dried mushrooms until soft, and cut off and discard the stems. Cut into julienne strips. Wash the *enoki* and cut off the tough ends. Stir-fry in 2 tablespoons oil until just done, then add ①. Mix well. This is the filling.

❷ Add ② to a wok and bring to a boil. Strain. This is the seasoning sauce.

❸ Brush some seasoning sauce over each sheet of bean curd skin (illus. 1). Stack the ten sheets together. Place the filling in the center of the top sheet, then roll into a 15×5 cm (6″×2″) cylinder (illus. 2). Place in a steamer and steam 5 minutes over high heat. Remove and allow to cool. This is the "vegetarian goose".

❹ Heat the remaining oil, then gently slide the vegetarian goose into it and deep-fry until golden. Remove from the oil and drain. Cut into 2 cm (¾″) wide pieces, arrange on a serving platter, and serve.

6人份
SERVES 6

香酥吉塊

Batter-Fried Mushrooms

材料：

洋菇⋯⋯⋯⋯ 300公克

① {
麵粉⋯⋯⋯⋯⋯ 1杯
水⋯⋯⋯⋯⋯⋯ ⅓杯
麻油⋯⋯⋯⋯ 1大匙
玉米粉⋯⋯⋯ 1大匙
塩、味精⋯⋯ ½小匙
胡椒粉⋯⋯⋯⋯少許
蛋⋯⋯⋯⋯⋯ 1個
}

❶①料調成麵糊備用，洋菇洗淨，川燙漂涼（圖一）備用。

❷炸油燒7分熱（300°F），洋菇沾麵糊，入鍋炸成金黃色（圖二），食時沾椒塩或番茄醬即可。

INGREDIENTS:

300 g (⅔ lb.)		fresh mushrooms
① {	1 c.	flour
	⅓ c.	water
	1 T.	sesame oil
	1 T.	cornstarch
	½ t.	salt
	pinch	pepper
	1	egg

❶ Mix ① until smooth to make a batter. Wash the mushrooms, blanch briefly in boiling water, and cool in a bowl of tap water (illus. 1). Drain and set aside.

❷ Heat the oil to about 300°F (149°C). Dip the mushrooms in the batter and deep-fry until golden (illus. 2). Dip in pepper-salt or ketchup before eating.

6人份
SERVES 6

海棠百花菇

材料：

金菇	150公克		芹菜末	1大匙	
豆包末	100公克		薑末	1大匙	
荸薺末	20公克		麻油	1小匙	
紫菜皮	1張	①	塩、糖	各½小匙	
豆腐皮	1張		味精	½小匙	
炸油	6杯		胡椒粉	少許	
			蛋白	½個	
		②	麵粉	1大匙	
			水	½大匙	

❶金菇去頭部洗淨切2公分長段，與豆包末、荸薺末
及①料拌勻成餡備用。

❷豆腐皮攤開，紫菜皮置其上，將餡放在紫菜中間，
包捲成12×12公分之正方形，接口以②料粘緊，入蒸
籠以大火蒸30分鐘，取出是爲海棠，待涼切2公分
寬斜片勿斷(圖一)，再與切紋交叉，斜切2公分寬
(圖二)。

❸炸油燒8分熱(350°F)，將海棠炸成金黃色，撈起
瀝油排盤即成。食時可沾番茄醬。

Flowers in Bloom

INGREDIENTS:

150 g (⅓ lb.)	*enoki* (golden mushrooms)
100 g (3½ oz.)	bean curd pocket, minced
20 g (⅔ oz.)	water chestnuts, minced
1 sheet	purple laver
1 sheet	bean curd skin
6 c.	oil for frying
① 1 T. each:	minced Chinese celery, minced ginger root
1 t.	sesame oil
½ t. each:	salt, sugar
pinch	pepper
½	egg white
② 1 T.	flour
½ T.	water

❶ Trim the tough ends off the *enoki*, wash, and cut into 2 cm
(¾″) lengths. Mix with the minced bean curd pocket,
minced water chestnut, and ① to make a filling.

❷ Spread the bean curd skin open, and lay the sheet of
purple laver seaweed on top of it. Place the filling in the
middle of the purple laver, then wrap into a 12×12 cm
(4¾″ × 4¾″) square. Seal the opening tightly with ②. Steam
over high heat for 30 minutes. Allow to cool, then make a
series of parallel diagonal slashes 2 cm (¾″) apart. Do not
cut all the way through (illus. 1). Make another series of
diagonal slashes crosswise to the first series, also at 2 cm
(¾″) intervals, forming diamonds (illus. 2).

❸ Heat the oil to about 350°F (177°C). Deep-fry the connected
diamonds until golden. Remove from the oil, drain, and
place on a serving platter. May be dipped in ketchup
before eating.

6人份
SERVES 6

炸墨鬚

材料：
鮑魚菇··········· 600公克
炸油················ 6杯

① ┌ 醬油膏········ 1大匙
  │ 麻油··········· 1小匙
  │ 味精··········· ½小匙
  └ 胡椒粉、塩··· 各少許

② ┌ 塩············ 1大匙
  │ 花椒粉········ ½小匙
  └ 味精·········· ½小匙

❶鮑魚菇入鍋川燙、漂冷後去蒂切成佛手狀(圖一)，
　捏乾水份(圖二)與①料醃約10分鐘備用。
❷炸油燒7分熱(約300°F)，以大火將鮑魚菇入鍋炸
　成金黃色，撈起瀝油排盤即成。
❸②料炒熟成椒塩，食時沾椒塩味道更佳。

Fried Abalone Mushrooms

INGREDIENTS:
600 g (1⅓ lb.)   abalone mushrooms
6 c.   oil for frying

① ┌ 1 T.   thick soy sauce
  │ 1 t.   sesame oil
  └ pinch each: pepper, salt

② ┌ 1 T.   salt
  └ ½ t.   ground Szechuan pepper,

❶ Blanch the abalone mushrooms briefly in boiling water. Cool in a bowl of tap water. Remove the stems and fringe into ''Buddha's hands'' (illus. 1). Squeeze out the excess moisture (illus. 2). Marinate in ① for 10 minutes.
❷ Heat the oil to about 300°F (149°C). Deep-fry the mushrooms until golden over high heat. Remove from the oil, drain, and arrange on a serving platter.
❸ Roast ② in a dry wok, stirring around constantly to prevent scorching. Dip the mushrooms in this pepper-salt mixture before eating for extra flavor.

6人份
SERVES 6

脆皮桃酥

材料：

核桃	100公克	
豆皮	6張	① { 白芝麻 …… 2大匙
炸油	6杯	{ 糖 …… 1大匙

❶將核桃切成細末，與①料入鍋拌炒數下成餡，再分成12等分備用。

❷豆皮對切共12張，每小張豆皮放1份餡，捲包起來(圖一)，再打結(圖二)共12個。

❸炸油燒7分熱(約300°F)，入鍋炸至金黃色撈起瀝油即成。

Walnut-Sesame Crisps

INGREDIENTS:

100 g (3½ oz.)	walnuts
6 sheets	bean curd skin
6 c.	oil for frying
① { 2 T.	white sesame seeds
{ 1 T.	sugar

❶ Mince the walnuts finely. Toast in a dry wok with ①, stirring constantly to prevent scorching. This is the walnut-sesame filling. Divide into 12 equal portions.

❷ Cut each of the 6 sheets of bean curd skin in half to make 12 small sheets. Place one portion of walnut-sesame filling in each small sheet of bean curd skin, wrap as shown (illus. 1), and tie (illus. 2).

❸ Heat the oil to about 300°F (149°C) and deep-fry the packets until golden. Remove from the oil, drain, and arrange on a serving plate.

6人份
SERVES 6

油炸馬鈴薯

Potato Croquettes

材料：

馬鈴薯·············	200公克		塩、味精······½小匙
罐頭玉米粒········	60公克	①	蛋················1個
罐頭豌豆仁········	40公克		胡椒粉··········少許
芹菜末·············	1大匙		麵包粉、太白粉···各 1杯
蛋····················	1個		
炸油················	6杯		

❶馬鈴薯去皮切片蒸熟，入①料、玉米粒、豌豆仁及
　芹菜末一起拌匀後，分成６等份，將每份馬鈴薯泥
　捏成直徑３公分，高３公分的圓柱形（圖一）備用。
❷炸油燒６分熱（約250°Ｆ），蛋打散成蛋液，依先後
　次序將❶料沾上太白粉、蛋液及麵包粉（圖二），再
　入鍋炸成金黃色撈出瀝油即成。

INGREDIENTS:

200 g (7 oz.)		potatoes
60 g (2 oz.)		canned whole kernel corn
40 g (1½ oz.)		canned (or frozen) peas
1 T.		minced Chinese celery
1		egg
6 c.		oil for frying
①	½ t.	salt
	1	egg
	pinch	pepper
	1 c. each:	fine bread crumbs, cornstarch

❶ Pare the potatoes, slice, and steam until soft.
Add ①, the corn, the peas, and the minced
celery. Mash and stir until well blended.
Divide into 6 equal portions. Mold each
portion into a 3 cm (1¼″) long and 3 cm
(1¼″) diameter cylinder shape (illus. 1).
❷ Heat the oil to about 250°F (121°C). Beat the
egg lightly. Dip the croquettes first in the
cornstarch, then the egg, and finally the fine
bread crumbs (illus. 2). Deep-fry until golden.
Remove from the oil, drain, and place on a
serving plate.

6人份
SERVES 6

烤素鰻

Fried Vegetarian Eel

材料：

紫菜皮	2張		塩	⅛小匙
豆包	2個	②	味精	⅛小匙 二份
檸檬	¼個		胡椒粉	少許
炸油	6杯		醬油膏	1小匙

①{
麵粉 1杯
水 ½杯
沙拉油 1大匙
塩、味精 各少許
蛋 1個
}

③{
醬油膏 1小匙
細糖、酒 各1小匙
白芝麻 少許
}

❶①料拌勻成麵糊備用。

❷紫菜皮一張攤開，上抹1大匙麵糊（圖一），攤開一個豆包置紫菜皮中間，再灑上一份②料，將紫菜皮捲成6公分寬的長條形（圖二），另一份也同樣處理，共做成二條素鰻。

❸炸油燒7分熱（300°F），將素鰻沾麵糊入鍋炸至金黃色，取出瀝油切成3公分寬片排盤即成。

❹食時將檸檬擠汁，淋在上面沾③料食用即成。

INGREDIENTS:

2 sheets		purple laver seaweed	
2		bean curd pockets	
¼		lemon	
6 c.		oil for frying	

①{
1 c. flour
½ c. water
1 T. oil
pinch salt
1 egg
}

②{
⅛ t. salt (prepare 2 portions)
pinch pepper
}

③{
1 t. each: thick soy sauce, fine sugar, rice wine
white sesame seeds, as needed
}

❶ Blend ① into a smooth batter.

❷ Open up a sheet of purple laver and spread on 1 tablespoon of batter (illus. 1). Open up one of the bean curd pockets and place it in the center of the purple laver. Sprinkle on a portion of ❷. Roll the purple laver into a 6 cm (2½″) wide cylinder shape (illus. 2). Follow the same procedure for the remaining ingredients. These are the two vegetarian ''eels''.

❸ Heat the oil to about 300°F (149°C). Dip the ''eels'' into the batter and deep-fry until golden. Remove from the oil, drain, and cut into 3 cm (1¼″) pieces. Arrange on a serving plate.

❹ Squeeze some lemon juice over the ''eels'' and dip in ③ before eating.

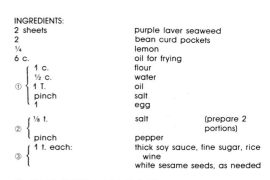

6人份
SERVES 6

蔬菜天婦羅

Vegetable Tempura

材料：

台生菜葉	3片	麵粉	1杯
新鮮香菇片	70公克	冰水	⅔杯
青椒片	50公克	① 沙拉油	1大匙
蘋果片	50公克	塩、味精	各¼小匙
炸油	6杯	蛋黃	1個
		② 白蘿蔔泥	1大匙
		醬油	1大匙
		糖	1小匙
		塩、味精	各¼小匙

❶①料調成麵糊以篩網過篩，生菜葉洗淨去葉梗瀝乾均備用。

❷炸油燒7分熱（300°Ｆ）關小火，將⅔的麵糊以手抓取，快速灑在油鍋上（圖一），使之變成絲狀連在一起之麵餅後，速將生菜葉、香菇片、青椒片、蘋果片，分別排於其上（圖二），最後將剩餘的麵糊以同法續灑在這些蔬菜上，待麵糊炸酥脆即取出切6小塊，再回鍋大火炸1分鐘，撈起瀝乾，食時沾②料即成。

■排盤時上可灑一些炸過的冬粉及紫菜以增加美觀。

6人份
SERVES 6

INGREDIENTS:

3 leaves		lettuce
70 g (2½ oz.)		fresh Chinese black mushrooms, sliced
50 g (1¾ oz.) each:		green pepper slices, apple slices
6 c.		oil for frying
	1 c.	flour
	⅔ c.	ice water
①	1 T.	oil
	¼ t.	salt
	1	egg yolk
	1 T. each:	Chinese white radish puree, soy sauce
②	1 t.	sugar
	¼ t.	salt

❶ Blend ① into a smooth batter and pass through a strainer. Wash the lettuce leaves, cut off the tough stem portion, and drain well.

❷ Heat the oil to about 300°F (149°C), then turn the heat to low. With your hand, scoop up about ⅔ of the batter and quickly drizzle it into the hot oil (illus. 1) so that it fries into linked ribbons. Immediately place the lettuce leaves, mushroom slices, green pepper slices, and apple slices on the frying batter (illus. 2). Finally, drizzle the remaining batter over the top of the vegetables in the same way as for the first portion. Deep-fry until crisp and golden. Remove from the oil, cut into 6 equally-sized pieces, and return to the oil to deep-fry over high heat another minute. Remove from the oil and drain well. Dip in ② before eating.

■ A little deep-fried bean thread and purple laver may be sprinkled over the top of the fried vegetables before serving to make them extra attractive.

三丁蝦仁

Shrimp Stir-Fry

材料：

素蝦仁	200公克	水	1½杯
紅蘿蔔	80公克 ①	塩、味精	½小匙
毛豆	60公克	糖、胡椒粉	各少許
香菇	10公克	水	1大匙
芹菜末	1大匙 ②	麻油	1小匙
油	2大匙	太白粉	1小匙

❶ 香菇泡軟去蒂，切1公分立方塊 (圖一) 備用。紅蘿蔔去皮亦切1公分立方塊，與洗淨後的毛豆同入鍋燙熟備用。

❷ 鍋熱入油2大匙，入香菇丁爆香，再入紅蘿蔔丁、毛豆及素蝦仁拌炒數下，後入①料拌勻並煮沸，以②料勾芡 (圖二)，起鍋前灑上芹菜末即成。

INGREDIENTS:

200 g (7 oz.)		vegetarian shrimp
80 g (3 oz.)		carrot
60 g (2 oz.)		fresh soybeans (or peas)
10 g (⅓ oz.)		dried Chinese black mushrooms
1 T.		minced Chinese celery
2 T.		oil
①	1½ c.	water
	½ t.	salt
	pinch each:	sugar, pepper
②	1 T.	water
	1 t.	sesame oil
	1 t.	cornstarch

❶ Soak the mushrooms until soft and remove the stems. Cut into 1 cm (⅜") cubes (illus. 1) and set aside. Pare the carrot and also cut into 1 cm (⅜") cubes. Wash the fresh soybeans. Immerse the carrot and fresh soybeans in boiling water until cooked through.

❷ Add 2 tablespoons oil to a preheated wok. and stir-fry the mushroom briefly. Next add the carrot, fresh soybeans, and vegetarian shrimp, and continue to stir-fry. Add ①, stir until well combined, and bring to a boil. Add ② to thicken (illus. 2). Sprinkle the minced Chinese celery over the top, then transfer to a serving dish and serve.

6人份
SERVES 6

四色素燴

Four-Color Vegie Platter

材料：

草菇‥‥‥‥‥	200公克		
青江菜‥‥‥‥‥	12棵	②	水‥‥‥‥‥ 1½杯
玉米筍‥‥‥‥‥	4支		塩、味精‥各½小匙
番茄‥‥‥‥‥	1個		胡椒粉‥‥‥‥少許
①	水‥‥‥‥‥½杯	③	水‥‥‥‥‥ 1大匙
	醬油‥‥‥‥1大匙		太白粉‥‥‥ 1小匙
	糖、麻油‥各1 小匙		麻油‥‥‥‥ 1大匙

❶青江菜洗淨去老葉修齊（圖一），玉米筍對切成二半，分別入沸水中川燙，撈起漂涼備用。

❷草菇去蒂頭與①料入鍋，以小火燒至水份略乾，盛起備用。

❸番茄1個去蒂等切成8小片，去皮及籽（圖二）與青江菜、玉米筍、草菇同排入盤中。

❹②料入鍋煮沸，以③料勾芡，起鍋前灑上麻油，盛起淋在蔬菜上即成。

INGREDIENTS:

200 g (7 oz.)			straw mushrooms
12 small stalks			*ching kang tsai* (or other stalk greens)
4 cobs			baby corn
1			tomato
①	{	½ c.	water
		1 T.	soy sauce
		1 t. each:	sugar, sesame oil
②	{	1½ c.	water
		½ t.	salt
		pinch	pepper
③	{	1 T.	water
		1 t.	cornstarch
		1 T.	sesame oil

❶ Wash the *ching kang tsai* (or other greens), remove the tough and wilted leaves, and trim to an even length (illus. 1). Halve the baby corn lengthwise. Blanch the greens and baby corn separately in boiling water. Remove and cool in tap water.

❷ Remove the stems from the straw mushrooms. Place the mushrooms in a wok with ① and heat over a low flame until most of the liquid has evaporated. Place in a bowl and set aside.

❸ Cut the stem out from the tomato, then cut into 8 equal wedges. Peel and seed (illus. 2). Arrange on a serving platter with the greens, baby corn, and straw mushrooms.

❹ Add ② to the wok and bring to a boil. Add ③ to thicken. Sprinkle on the sesame oil, then pour over the vegetable platter and serve.

6人份
SERVES 6

口磨燴絲瓜

Luffa Gourd with Mushrooms

材料：

絲瓜················1200公克		水·················½杯	
罐頭洋菇········ 180公克		味精、醬油··· 1小匙	
薑末················ 1大匙	①	番茄醬········ 1小匙	
辣椒末············· 1小匙		麻油··········· 1小匙	
炸油················· 2杯		糖、塩·····各½小匙	
塩·················¼小匙	②	水·············½大匙	
		太白粉········½小匙	

❶絲瓜去薄皮，對剖兩半後切成５公分長段，去掉白色部份（圖一），將青的部份切成細絲，入開水中煮３分鐘，撈起，加¼小匙塩拌勻圍盤備用。

❷洋菇每個均以斜刀雕成"╳"狀（圖二），炸油２杯燒熱，入洋菇稍炸即撈起備用。

❸鍋內留油２大匙燒熱，爆香紅椒末、薑末後，入洋菇及①料煮１分鐘，再以②料勾芡，淋於絲瓜上，食時拌勻即成。

INGREDIENTS:

1200 g (2⅔ lb.)		luffa gourd (loofah, dishcloth gourd, *see kwa*)
180 g (6 oz.)		canned mushrooms
1 T.		minced ginger root
1 t.		minced red chili pepper
2 c.		oil for frying
¼ t.		salt
①	½ c.	water
	1 t. each:	soy sauce, ketchup, sesame oil
	½ t. each:	sugar, salt
②	½ T.	water
	½ t.	cornstarch

❶ Pare the luffa gourd and halve lengthwise. Cut into 5 cm (2″) segments. Scoop out the white portion (illus. 1), then shred the green portion. Immerse in boiling water 3 minutes and remove. Mix in ¼ teaspoon salt, then arrange on a serving plate.

❷ Holding the knife at an angle, carve a ✳ figure onto the cap of each mushroom (illus. 2). Heat the 2 cups of oil for frying, then deep-fry the mushrooms briefly. Remove from the oil and set aside.

❸ Pour off all but 2 tablespoons oil from the wok and heat. Fry the minced red chili pepper and the minced ginger root until fragrant. Add the mushrooms and ①. Allow to cook for 1 minute, then add ② to thicken. Pour over the shredded luffa gourd. Mix well before eating.

6人份
SERVES 6

大燴海參

Sea Cucumber in Sauce

材料：

素海參··········	130公克	油··············	2大匙
鮑魚菇··········	100公克	┌ 水············	1½杯
小黃瓜··········	100公克	│ 醬油··········	1大匙
玉米筍··········	70公克	① ┤ 糖、味精······	少許
熟紅蘿蔔片·······	30公克	└ 胡椒粉·········	少許
熟綠竹筍片·······	30公克	┌ 水············	2大匙
香菇············	10公克	② ┤ 太白粉·····	1½小匙
薑末、芹菜末···各	1大匙	└ 麻油·········	1大匙

❶素海參、鮑魚菇洗淨切片，玉米筍每支斜切成2段，小黃瓜去皮切段（圖一），再將每段切成3片並去籽（圖二），香菇泡軟去蒂切片均備用。

❷鍋熱入油2大匙，爆香薑末，入❶料同炒數下，加①料燜煮5分鐘，再以②料勾芡，起鍋前加紅蘿蔔片、綠竹筍片灑上芹菜末即成。

INGREDIENTS:

130 g (4½ oz.)	vegetarian sea cucumber
100 g (3½ oz.)	abalone mushrooms
100 g (3½ oz.)	gherkin cucumbers
70 g (2½ oz.)	baby corn
30 g (1 oz.) each:	cooked carrot slices, bamboo shoot slices
10 g (⅓ oz.)	dried Chinese black mushrooms
1 T. each:	minced ginger root, minced Chinese celery
2 T.	oil
① ⎰ 1½ c.	water
⎱ 1 T.	soy sauce
⎱ pinch each:	sugar, pepper
② ⎰ 2 T.	water
⎱ 1½ t.	cornstarch
⎱ 1 T.	sesame oil

❶ Wash the vegetarian sea cucumber and abalone mushrooms, and slice. Cut each cob of baby corn diagonally into two segments. Pare the gherkin cucumber and cut into segments (illus. 1), then cut each segment into 3 slices and scrape out the seeds (illus. 2). Soak the dried Chinese black mushrooms until soft, remove the stems, and slice.

❷ Preheat a wok, then add 2 tablespoons oil. Fry the minced ginger until fragrant, add the ingredients in step ① and the carrot and bamboo slices, and stir-fry briefly. Add ❶, simmer covered for 5 minutes, then thicken with ❷. Sprinkle the minced Chinese celery over the top, transfer to a serving dish, and serve.

6人份
SERVES 6

一品排翅

Shark Fins Deluxe

材料：

綠竹筍⋯⋯ 淨重300公克		醬油⋯⋯⋯⋯ 1大匙
蒟蒻片⋯⋯⋯⋯80公克		麻油⋯⋯⋯⋯ 1大匙
紅蘿蔔片⋯⋯⋯⋯70公克	①	番茄醬⋯⋯⋯ ½大匙
香菇片⋯⋯⋯⋯70公克		糖、味精⋯各½小匙
洋菇片⋯⋯⋯⋯70公克		水⋯⋯⋯⋯⋯⋯ 1杯
芹菜末、薑末⋯⋯各1小匙	②	麻油⋯⋯⋯⋯ 1小匙
炸油⋯⋯⋯⋯⋯⋯ 3杯		塩、味精⋯各½小匙
	③	水⋯⋯⋯⋯⋯ 1大匙
		太白粉⋯⋯⋯ ⅔小匙

❶綠竹筍切４×５公分長片，每片再切成佛手狀（圖一）；炸油燒８分熱（約350°Ｆ），入筍片炸成金黃色撈起瀝油備用。

❷鍋內留油少許，爆香薑末、芹菜末再入紅蘿蔔、香菇、洋菇、蒟蒻片及炸好之綠竹筍，拌炒均勻即入①料燜煮５分鐘，再倒入扣碗，並以大火蒸５分鐘，取出倒扣在盤中（圖二）備用。

❸②料燒開，以③料勾芡，淋在❷上即成。

INGREDIENTS:

300 g (⅔ lb.)		fresh bamboo shoots (husked)
80 g (3 oz.)		*konnyaku* slices
70 g (2½ oz.) each:		carrot slices, dried Chinese black mushroom slices, fresh mushroom slices
1 t. each:		minced Chinese celery, minced ginger root
3 c.		oil for frying
①	1 T. each:	soy sauce, sesame oil
	½ T.	ketchup
	½ t.	sugar
②	1 c.	water
	1 t.	sesame oil
	½ t.	salt
③	1 T.	water
	⅔ t.	cornstarch

❶ Cut the bamboo shoots into 4×5 cm (1½″×2″) slices. Fringe the slices to make "Buddha's hands" (illus. 1). Heat the oil for frying to about 350°F (177°C). Add the bamboo shoots to the oil and fry until golden. Remove from the oil and drain.

❷ Leave a small amount of oil in the wok. Fry the minced ginger root and minced Chinese celery until fragrant, then add the carrot, black mushroom, fresh mushroom, *konnyaku* slices, and the fried bamboo shoots. Stir-fry briefly until the ingredients are well combined. Add ① and simmer, covered, 5 minutes. Transfer to a bowl and steam 5 minutes over high heat. Invert onto a serving plate (illus. 2).

❸ Bring ② to a boil, thicken with ③, and pour over the mixture from step ❷. Serve.

6人份
SERVES 6

燴素春腦

材料：

白米	1杯	鮮奶	½杯
草菇片	100公克	玉米粉	½杯
新鮮香菇丁	70公克	① 塩、味精	各少許
紅棗(約10顆)	10公克	胡椒粉	少許
毛豆	¼杯	水	1杯
水	3杯	② 麻油	1小匙
油	2大匙	塩、味精	½小匙
		③ 水	1大匙
		太白粉	⅔小匙

❶ 白米洗淨，以３杯水泡２小時，入果汁機打成汁過濾（圖一），①料拌勻，再以中火邊煮邊攪拌至沸騰（圖二），即倒入扣碗中，再以大火蒸５分鐘，取出倒扣盤中是爲素腦。

❷ 紅棗先泡軟，鍋熱入油，再入紅棗、草菇片、香菇片及毛豆拌炒均勻，續入②料燒開，並以③料勾芡淋在素腦上即成。

Vegetarian Pork Brain

INGREDIENTS:

1 c.		raw white rice
100 g (3½ oz.)		straw mushrooms, sliced
70 g (2½ oz.)		fresh Chinese black mushrooms, diced
10 g (½ oz.)		dried Chinese red dates (about 10)
¼ c.		fresh soybeans (or peas)
3 c.		water
2 T.		oil
①	½ c. each:	fresh milk, *cornstarch*
	pinch each:	salt, pepper
②	1 c.	water
	1 t.	sesame oil
	½ t.	salt
③	1 T.	water
	⅔ t.	cornstarch

❶ Wash the rice, then soak 2 hours in 3 cups water. Liquefy in a blender and strain (illus. 1). Mix in ① until well blended. Bring to a boil over medium heat, stirring constantly (illus. 2). Pour into a bowl and steam 5 minutes over high heat. Invert onto a plate. This is the "vegetarian pork brain."

❷ Wash the dried Chinese red dates and soak until soft. Heat a wok and add the oil. Stir-fry the red dates, sliced straw mushrooms, sliced Chinese black mushrooms, and fresh soybeans together until well combined. Add ② and bring to a boil. Thicken with ③. Pour over the vegetarian pork brain and serve.

6人份
SERVES 6

三鮮鍋粑

Vegetables with Crispy Rice

材料：

鍋粑	6塊	薑	2片
豌豆片	8片	炸油	6杯
鮑魚菇	120公克	① 水	3杯
白豆干	100公克	酒、麻油…各	1大匙
素海參片	70公克	塩、味精…各	1小匙
紅蘿蔔片	50公克	② 水	3大匙
香菇	10公克	太白粉	1大匙
芹菜段	6段		

❶炸油燒熱，入鍋粑炸黃（圖一），撈起排盤備用；豌豆片去老梗也備用。

❷香菇泡軟洗淨與鮑魚菇均去蒂切斜片（圖二）備用，白豆干切長片，炸稍黃撈起備用。

❸鍋熱入油2大匙，爆香薑片及芹菜段，入❷料，紅蘿蔔片及素海參片一起拌炒均勻，再以①料燜煮數分鐘入豌豆片，最後以②料勾芡，起鍋淋於鍋粑上即成。

INGREDIENTS:

6 cakes	rice, fried crispy (kuo pa)
8	Chinese peapods
120 g (4 oz.)	abalone mushrooms
100 g (3½ oz.)	white pressed bean curd (tou kan)
70 g (2½ oz.)	vegetarian sea cucumber, sliced
50 g (1¾ oz.)	carrot slices
10 oz. (⅓ oz.)	dried Chinese black mushrooms
6 pieces	Chinese celery
2 slices	ginger root
6 c.	oil for frying
① { 3 c.	water
1 T. each:	rice wine, sesame oil
1 t.	salt
② { 3 T.	water
1 T.	cornstarch

❶ Heat the oil for frying. Add the rice cakes (kuo pa; rice that sticks to the bottom of the pot after cooking) and deep-fry until golden (illus. 1). Remove from the oil and place on a plate. Remove the ends and strings from the Chinese peapods.

❷ Soak the black mushrooms until soft and rinse clean. Remove and discard the stems from the black mushrooms and abalone mushrooms, then slice both diagonally. Cut the white pressed bean curd into long slices (illus. 2), then deep-fry briefly, until just beginning to turn golden.

❸ Heat a wok and add 2 tablespoons oil. Stir-fry the ginger root and celery briefly. Add the ingredients from step ❷, the carrot slices, and the vegetarian sea cucumber slices. Stir-fry until the ingredients are well combined. Pour in ① and simmer 2 minutes, covered. Add the Chinese peapods. Thicken with ②. Pour over the fried crisp rice cakes and serve.

6人份
SERVES 6

菜心竹笙

Bamboo Pith with Greens

材料：

竹笙·················10公克	
青江菜··········· 600公克	① { 水·················· 1杯 酒、麻油···各 1小匙 味精、塩···各 ½小匙
白果（罐頭）··········½杯	
薑末················· 1小匙	② { 水·············· 1大匙 太白粉········ 1小匙
油················· 2大匙	

❶竹笙泡軟、片開，切約4公分長段備用（圖一）。
❷青江菜洗淨，燙熟後漂涼瀝乾排盤備用（圖二）。
❸鍋熱入油，再爆香薑末，入竹笙、白果，炒熟再入
　①料拌炒數下，起鍋前以②料勾茨即可淋在排好青
　江菜的盤中。

INGREDIENTS:

10 g (⅓ oz.)	dried bamboo pith (*chu sheng*)
600 g (1⅓ lb.)	*ching kang tsai* (or other leafy stalk greens)
½ c.	gingko nuts
1 t.	minced ginger root
2 T.	oil
① { 1 c. 1 t. each: ½ t.	water rice wine, sesame oil salt
② { 1 T. 1 t.	water cornstarch

❶ Soak the bamboo pith until soft. Cut into pieces about 4 cm (1½″) long (illus. 1).
❷ Wash the greens, blanch briefly in boiling water, then cool in tap water. Drain well and arrange on a serving plate (illus. 2).
❸ Heat a wok and add the oil. Stir-fry the minced ginger root briefly, then add the bamboo pith and gingko nuts. Stir-fry until cooked through. Add ① and continue to stir-fry. Thicken with ②. Pour over the greens and serve.

6人份
SERVES 6

冬林羅漢 / Arhat's Feast

材料：

青江菜…………600公克	
紅蘿蔔、草菇…各40公克	
玉米筍……………30公克	
栗子………………30公克	
紅棗………………30公克	
小麵筋泡…………15公克	
白果（罐頭）………10公克	
香菇………………10公克	
蓮子………………10公克	
油…………………2大匙	

①
- 素高湯………2小匙
- 醬油…………2小匙
- 薑汁…………2小匙
- 味精…………½小匙
- 糖……………½小匙
- 塩、胡椒粉……少許

②
- 水……………1大匙
- 太白粉………⅔小匙
- 麻油…………少許

❶將蓮子、紅棗洗淨，以温水泡軟，栗子放碗中加水蓋滿，入蒸籠蒸熟；草菇洗淨去蒂頭對切成半，香菇泡軟去蒂，紅蘿蔔去皮與玉米筍均切2×1公分大小丁狀（圖二），青江菜去老葉，尾部修齊以開水川燙、漂涼均備用。

❷鍋熱入油2大匙，爆香香菇再入紅蘿蔔、玉米筍、草菇拌炒數下，續入蓮子、栗子、紅棗、白果同炒數分鐘，後入①料及小麵筋泡燜煮1分鐘，以②料勾茨後，再入青江菜拌勻，起鍋前將青江菜取出排盤圍邊（圖三），其餘材料置盤中即成。

■（圖一）爲本道菜餚所有使用材料

INGREDIENTS:

600 g (1⅓ lb.)	*ching kang tsai* (or other leafy stalk green)
40 g (1½ oz.) each:	carrot, straw mushrooms
30 g (1 oz.)	baby corn
30 g (1 oz.)	chestnuts (dried)
30 g (1 oz.)	dried Chinese red dates
15 g (½ oz.)	wheat gluten puffs (small)
10 g (⅓ oz.)	gingko nuts (canned)
10 g (⅓ oz.)	dried Chinese black mushrooms
10 g (⅓ oz.)	lotus seeds
2 T.	oil

①
2 t. each:	vegetarian stock, soy sauce, ginger root juice
½ t.	sugar
pinch each:	salt, pepper

②
1 T.	water
⅔ t.	cornstarch
dash	sesame oil

❶ Wash the lotus seeds and the Chinese red dates and soak in warm water until soft. Boil in water until cooked through. Place the dried chestnuts in a bowl, add water to cover, and steam until soft. Wash the straw mushrooms, cut off the stems, then halve lengthwise. Soak the Chinese black mushrooms until soft and remove the stems. Pare the carrot. Cut the carrot and baby corn into 2×1 cm (¾″ × ⅜″) bits (illus. 2). Remove the tough and wilted leaves from the greens, trim the ends so that they are even, and blanch briefly in boiling water. Cool in tap water.

❷ Heat a wok and add 2 tablespoons oil. Fry the black mushroom briefly, then add the carrot, baby corn, and straw mushrooms. Stir-fry until combined. Add the lotus seeds, chestnuts, red dates, and gingko nuts, and stir-fry several minutes. Add ① and the wheat gluten puffs. Cover and simmer 1 minute. Thicken with ②, then add the greens and stir until combined. Remove the greens and arrange them around the edge of a serving plate (illus. 3). Pour the remaining ingredients onto the center of the plate and serve.

■ Illustrated are the ingredients used to make this dish.

五味鮮魚

Five-Flavor Whole Fish

材料：

素魚·················· 1條		水··············· 1杯	
青椒絲···········50公克		烏醋··········· 2大匙	
紅蘿蔔絲·········50公克		醬油··········· 1大匙	
香菇絲···········50公克		番茄醬········· 1大匙	
筍絲·············50公克	①	糖、麻油····· 1小匙	
紅椒絲···········10公克		味精···········½小匙	
香菜末·············少許		胡椒粉·········½小匙	
炸油·············· 6杯		塩···············¼小匙	
	②	水··············· 1大匙	
		太白粉········· 1小匙	

❶在素魚上每隔1公分切斜連刀片（圖一），炸油燒7
　分熱（約300°F），將素魚炸成金黃色撈起瀝油排盤。

❷鍋內留油少許，入青椒絲、紅蘿蔔絲、香菇絲、筍
　絲（圖二）爆香，再入①料拌炒1分鐘，即以②料勾
　芡淋在素魚上，最後灑上紅椒絲及香菜末即成。

INGREDIENTS:

1	vegetarian fish
50 g (2 oz.)	green pepper, julienned
50 g (2 oz.)	carrot, julienned
50 g (2 oz.)	dried Chinese black mushrooms, soaked until soft and julienned
50 g (2 oz.)	bamboo shoots, julienned
10 g (⅓ oz.)	sweet red pepper, julienned
	minced fresh coriander (Chinese parsley; cilantro), as desired
6 c.	oil for frying
① 1 c.	water
2 T.	Chinese black vinegar
1 T each:	soy sauce, ketchup
1 t. each:	sugar, sesame oil
½ t.	pepper
¼ t.	salt
② 1 T.	water
1 t.	cornstarch

❶ Make diagonal slashes at 1 cm (½") intervals on the
vegetarian fish (illus. 1). Heat the oil for frying to
about 300°F (149°C). Deep-fry the fish until golden.
Remove from the oil, drain well, and place on a
serving plate.

❷ Pour off all but a small amount of the oil. Stir-fry the
green pepper, carrot, and black mushroom briefly
(illus. 2). Add ① and continue to stir-fry 1 minute.
Thicken with ②, then pour over the fish. Sprinkle
some shredded sweet red pepper and minced fresh
coriander over the top and serve.

6人份
SERVES 6

蜜汁菱角

Glazed Water Caltrops

材料：

菱角 (淨重)‥‥‥‥ 300公克	
熟白芝麻‥‥‥‥‥ 2小匙	
炸油‥‥‥‥‥‥‥‥ 6杯	

① {
麵粉‥‥‥‥‥‥ 1杯
水‥‥‥‥‥‥‥ ½杯
沙拉油‥‥‥‥ 1大匙
蛋‥‥‥‥‥‥‥ 1個
}

② {
水‥‥‥‥‥‥‥ ½杯
糖‥‥‥‥‥‥‥ 4大匙
}

❶菱角洗淨蒸熟，①料拌勻成麵糊均備用。

❷炸油燒7分熱（300°F），將菱角沾麵糊入鍋炸至金黃色撈起瀝油。

❸②料煮沸倒入菱角（圖一）拌炒數下，起鍋前灑上白芝麻（圖二）即成。

INGREDIENTS:

300 g (⅔ lb.)	water caltrops (*ling chiao*; net wt.)
2 t.	toasted white sesame seeds
6 c.	oil for frying

① {
1 c. — flour
½ c. — water
1 T. — oil '
1 — egg
}

② {
½ c. — water
4 T. — sugar
}

❶ Wash the water caltrops and steam until cooked through. Mix ① well to make a smooth batter.

❷ Heat the oil to about 300°F (149°C). Dip the water caltrops into the batter and deep-fry until golden. Remove from the oil and drain.

❸ Bring ② to a boil, then add the deep-fried water caltrops (illus. 1) and stir gently until coated. Sprinkle some toasted white sesame seeds over the top (illus. 2), transfer to a serving dish, and serve.

6人份
SERVES 6

金銀合瓣 — Gold, Silver and Jade

材料：

洋菇	300公克
高麗菜	200公克
黃茸	40公克
荸薺末	
玉米筍末	各1大匙
薑末	
罐頭白果	⅓杯
辣椒段	4段
沙拉醬	4大匙
炸油	4杯
辣豆瓣醬	⅔大匙

①
水	1杯
醬油	2小匙
酒釀	1小匙
麻油	1小匙
白醋	1小匙
糖、味精	各½小匙
塩	⅛小匙

②
水	1大匙
太白粉	1小匙

③
水	½杯
醬油	2小匙
糖、味精	各½小匙
塩	¼小匙

❶ 洋菇洗淨去蒂，黃茸泡約6小時後去蒂頭（圖一）備用。

❷ 炸油燒7分熱（約300°F），將洋菇炸熟撈起瀝油（圖二）；鍋內留油少許，爆香薑末、玉米筍末、荸薺末及辣豆瓣醬，即入①料及洋菇同煮數分鐘，再以½大匙的②料勾芡盛盤備用。

❸ 鍋熱入油2大匙，爆香辣椒段，即入黃茸拌炒數下，再入白菓及③料燜煮2分鐘後，以剩餘之②料勾芡盛盤備用。

❹ 高麗菜洗淨切細絲，置盤中央排成一長條形（圖三），上淋沙拉醬，兩側分別排上❷料及❸料即成。

Gold, Silver and Jade

INGREDIENTS:

300 g (⅔ lb.)	fresh mushrooms
200 g (7 oz.)	cabbage
40 g (1½ oz.)	edible yellow fungus (*huang jung*)
1 T. each:	minced water chestnuts, minced baby corn, minced ginger root
⅓ c.	canned gingko nuts
4 pieces	chili pepper
4 T.	mayonaise
4 c.	oil for frying
⅔ T.	hot bean paste

①
1 c.	water
2 t.	soy sauce
1 t. each:	sweet fermented rice (*chiu niang*), sesame oil, rice vinegar
½ t.	sugar
⅛ t.	salt

②
1 T.	water
1 t.	cornstarch

③
½ c.	water
2 t.	soy sauce
½ t.	sugar
¼ t.	salt

❶ Wash the fresh mushrooms and remove the stems. Soak the edible yellow fungus about 6 hours, then remove the tough ends (illus. 1).

❷ Heat the oil to about 300°F (149°C). Deep-fry the fresh mushrooms until cooked through, remove from the oil, and drain (illus. 2). Pour off all but a small amount of the oil from the wok. Fry the minced ginger root, minced baby corn, minced water chestnuts, and hot bean paste in the oil, then add ① and the mushrooms. Mix together and cook several minutes. Thicken by stirring in ½ tablespoon of ②. Transfer to a plate.

❸ Heat a wok and add 2 tablespoons oil. Fry the chili pepper briefly, then add the edible yellow fungus and stir several times. Add the gingko nuts and ③ and continue to heat 2 minutes, covered. Thicken with the rest of ②, and transfer to a plate.

❹ Wash the cabbage and shred. Arrange in a long mound on a serving plate (illus. 3) and top with some mayonaise. Place the ingredients prepared in steps ❷ and ❸ on either side of the shredded cabbage. Serve.

吉米瓜盅

Cashew Chicken in Whole Cantaloupe

材料：

哈蜜瓜⋯⋯⋯⋯⋯⋯ 1個		
素鷄⋯⋯⋯⋯⋯ 100公克	①	酒、麻油⋯各½大匙
小黃瓜⋯⋯⋯⋯ 100公克		醬油 ⋯⋯⋯⋯ 1小匙
紅蘿蔔⋯⋯⋯⋯⋯80公克		糖、味精⋯各½小匙
草菇⋯⋯⋯⋯⋯⋯70公克		塩⋯⋯⋯⋯⋯⋯¼小匙
炸好的腰果⋯⋯⋯⋯½杯	②	水⋯⋯⋯⋯⋯⋯ 1大匙
芹菜末⋯⋯⋯⋯⋯ 1大匙		太白粉⋯⋯⋯⋯½小匙
油⋯⋯⋯⋯⋯⋯⋯ 2大匙		

❶哈蜜瓜由中間以小刀切鋸齒狀（圖一），剝成二半（圖二），並去籽備用；素鷄、小黃瓜洗淨均切１公分大小之丁狀備用。

❷紅蘿蔔去皮切１公分大小丁，草菇洗淨對切成二半（圖三），分別入鍋以開水川燙撈起漂涼瀝乾備用。

❸鍋熱入油２大匙，爆香素鷄再入紅蘿蔔、小黃瓜及草菇拌炒數下，續入①料拌勻後，以②料勾芡灑上芹菜末盛起備用。

❹哈蜜瓜入蒸籠以大火蒸３分鐘後將❸料倒入續蒸１分鐘，取出灑上腰果，趁熱供食。

INGREDIENTS:

1		whole cantaloupe
100 g (3½ oz.)		vegetarian chicken
100 g (3½ oz.)		gherkin cucumber
80 g (3 oz.)		carrot
70 g (2½ oz.)		straw mushrooms
½ c.		deep-fried cashew nuts
1 T.		minced Chinese celery
2 T.		oil
①	½ T. each:	rice wine, sesame oil
	1 t.	soy sauce
	½ t.	sugar
	¼ t.	salt
②	1 T.	water
	½ t.	cornstarch

❶ Use a paring knife to cut the cantaloupe in half in a saw-toothed pattern (illus. 1,2). Remove the seeds. Cut the vegetarian chicken and gherkin cucumber into 1 cm (⅜") cubes.

❷ Pare the carrot and cut into 1 cm (⅜") cubes. Wash the straw mushrooms and halve lengthwise (illus. 3). Blanch each separately in boiling water, remove, and cool in tap water. Drain.

❸ Heat a wok and add 2 tablespoons oil. Fry the vegetarian chicken in the oil briefly, then add the carrot, gherkin cucumber, and straw mushrooms. Stir-fry briefly. Mix in first ①, then ② to thicken. Sprinkle the minced celery over the top, and transfer to a plate.

❹ Steam the cantaloupe halves 3 minutes over high heat, then pour half of the ingredients prepared in step ❸ into each half of the cantaloupe. Steam another minute. Remove from the steamer, sprinkle the cashews over the top, and serve hot.

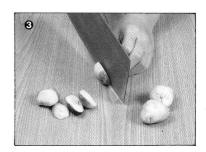

金菇仙糊

材料：

金菇	200公克		水	1大匙	
香菇	30公克		醬油、麻油	1小匙	
芹菜末	1大匙	①	薑汁	1小匙	
薑絲	1大匙		味精、糖	各½小匙	
油	2大匙		胡椒粉、塩	少許	
		②	水	1大匙	
			太白粉	⅔小匙	

❶金菇洗淨去頭（圖一），香菇泡軟去蒂切絲均備用。
❷鍋熱入油２大匙，爆香薑絲，即入香菇絲（圖二）及
　金菇拌炒數下，再入①料拌勻，最後以②料勾芡，
　起鍋前灑上芹菜末即成。

Ebony and Ivory

INGREDIENTS:

200 g (7 oz.)	*enoki* (golden mushrooms)
30 g (1 oz.)	dried Chinese black mushrooms
1 T.	minced Chinese celery
1 T.	shredded ginger root
2 T.	oil

	1 T.	water
	1 t. each:	soy sauce, sesame oil
①	1 t.	ginger root juice
	½ t.	sugar
	pinch each:	salt, pepper
②	1 T.	water
	⅔ t.	cornstarch

❶ Wash the *enoki* and trim off the ends (illus. 1).
Soak the Chinese black mushrooms until soft,
remove the stems, and shred.

❷ Heat a wok and add 2 tablespoons oil. Fry the
shredded ginger root briefly, then add the
shredded black mushroom (illus. 2) and the
enoki, and stir-fry briefly. Add ①, mixing
thoroughly, then thicken with ②. Sprinkle on
the minced Chinese celery, transfer to a
plate, and serve.

6人份
SERVES 6

金菇三絲

材料：

竹筍⋯⋯⋯⋯	120公克		酒⋯⋯⋯⋯	1小匙
銀芽⋯⋯⋯⋯	100公克	①	塩⋯⋯⋯⋯	½小匙
金菇⋯⋯⋯⋯	80公克		味精⋯⋯⋯	½小匙
紅蘿蔔⋯⋯⋯	60公克		胡椒粉⋯⋯⋯	少許
青椒⋯⋯⋯⋯	50公克			
油⋯⋯⋯⋯	2大匙			

❶紅蘿蔔、竹筍煮熟去皮去殼（圖一），均切５公分長絲備用。

❷銀芽、金菇、青椒均洗淨，金菇去頭，青椒去籽（圖二），切絲均備用。

❸鍋熱入油２大匙，將紅蘿蔔絲、筍絲、銀芽、金菇、青椒絲入鍋炒熟，再入①料拌勻即成。

Stir-Fry Julienne

INGREDIENTS:

120 g (¼ lb.)	bamboo shoots
100 g (3½ oz.)	mung bean sprouts (both ends removed)
80 g (3 oz.)	*enoki* (golden mushrooms)
60 g (2 oz.)	carrot
50 g (1¾ oz.)	green pepper
2 T.	oil
① { 1 t.	rice wine
½ t.	salt
pinch	pepper

❶ Cook the carrot and bamboo shoots until done. Pare the carrot and husk the bamboo shoots (illus. 1). Cut into 5 cm (2″) long julienne strips.

❷ Wash the mung bean sprouts, the *enoki*, and the green pepper. Trim the ends off the *enoki*. Seed the green pepper (illus. 2) and cut into julienne strips.

❸ Heat a wok and add 2 tablespoons oil. Add the carrot, bamboo shoots, bean sprouts, *enoki*, and green pepper, and stir-fry until just done. Mix in ① until the ingredients are well-coated. Serve.

6人份
SERVES 6

金菇百頁

Enoki With Bean Curd Sheet

材料：

百頁	10張	②	{ 水	4杯
金菇	80公克		{ 塩	1大匙
毛豆	2大匙	③	{ 塩、味精…各½小匙
油	2大匙		{ 麻油	少許
①	{ 温水 4杯	④	{ 水	½大匙
	{ 鹼塊 ¼小塊		{ 太白粉	½大匙

❶ 百頁切4×6公分（圖一），入①料泡約15分鐘（圖二），以②料沖洗乾淨；金菇洗淨去頭均備用。

❷ 鍋熱入油2大匙，將金菇、毛豆入鍋同炒數下後，入百頁及③料拌炒，並以④料勾芡即成。

INGREDIENTS:

10		bean curd sheets (*pai yeh*)
80 g (3 oz.)		*enoki* (golden mushrooms)
2 T.		fresh soybeans
2 T.		oil
①	{ 4 c.	warm water
	{ 1 t.	baking soda
②	{ 4 c.	water
	{ 1 T.	salt
③	{ ½ t.	salt
	{ dash	sesame oil
④	{ ½ T.	water
	{ ½ T.	cornstarch

❶ Cut the bean curd sheets into 4×6 cm (1½″×2¼″) pieces (illus. 1). Soak in ① about 15 minutes (illus. 2). Rinse clean with ②. Wash the *enoki* and trim off the ends.

❷ Heat a wok and add 2 tablespoons oil. Stir-fry the *enoki* and fresh soybeans briefly. Add the bean curd sheets and ③ and continue to stir-fry. Thicken with ④ and serve.

6人份
SERVES 6

# 翡翠菜鬆	# Vegetable Rolls

材料：

豆苗‥‥‥‥‥‥‥‥ 120公克　　炸油‥‥‥‥‥‥‥‥‥‥ 4杯

玉米筍末‥‥‥‥‥‥60公克　① ｛塩、味精‥各¼小匙

紅蘿蔔末‥‥‥‥‥‥60公克　　　醬油‥‥‥‥‥ 1大匙

荸薺末‥‥‥‥‥‥‥40公克　　　麻油‥‥‥‥‥ 1小匙

洋菇‥‥‥‥‥‥‥‥40公克　② ｛糖、味精‥各½小匙

香菇‥‥‥‥‥‥‥‥15公克　　　塩‥‥‥‥‥‥¼小匙

冬粉‥‥‥‥‥‥‥‥‥ 1把　　　烏醋‥‥‥‥‥ 少許

春捲皮‥‥‥‥‥‥‥ 6張

❶香菇泡軟去蒂，與洋菇均切末，豆苗去老莖洗淨（
　圖一），冬粉切５公分長段均備用。

❷炸油燒８分熱（350°F），入冬粉炸至膨脹（圖二）即
　撈起瀝油；鍋內留油少許，炒熟豆苗即入①料拌勻
　盛盤，並將冬粉置其上。

❸鍋熱入油１大匙，炒熟香菇末、洋菇末、荸薺末、
　玉米筍末及紅蘿蔔末，再入②料拌勻，盛盤置冬粉
　上是為菜鬆，食時以春捲皮包菜鬆即成。

INGREDIENTS:

120 g (¼ lb.)	peavine greens
60 g (2 oz.)	minced baby corn
60 g (2 oz.)	minced carrot
40 g (1½ oz.)	minced water chestnuts
40 g (1½ oz.)	fresh mushrooms
15 g (½ oz.)	dried Chinese black mushrooms
1 bunch	bean thread (fun see)
6	eggroll wrappers (thin)
4 c.	oil for frying
① ¼ t.	salt
1 T.	soy sauce
1 t.	sesame oil
② ½ t.	sugar
¼ t.	salt
dash	Chinese dark vinegar

❶ Soak the dried Chinese black mushrooms until soft and remove the stems. Mince the black and fresh mushrooms. Discard the tough portions of the peavine greens and wash (illus. 1). Cut the bean thread into 5 cm (2″) lengths.

❷ Heat the oil to about 350°F (177°C). Fry the bean thread until it puffs up (illus. 2). Remove from the oil and drain. Pour off all but a small amount of the oil in the wok. Stir-fry the peavine greens until just done. Mix in ① well, then transfer to a plate. Place the fried bean thread on top of the greens.

❸ Heat a wok and add 1 tablespoon oil. Stir-fry the minced black mushroom, minced fresh mushroom, minced water chestnut, minced baby corn and minced carrot briefly. Add ② and combine well. Pour over the top of the fried bean thread. Each guest wraps some of the minced vegetable, bean thread, and greens in an eggroll wrapper to eat.

6人份
SERVES 6

茄汁元寶

Filled Nuggets in Tomato Sauce

材料：

罐頭荔枝	1罐	
馬鈴薯	80公克	
紅蘿蔔	70公克	
罐頭鳳梨片	70公克	
青椒片	50公克	
炸油	6杯	

① 麵粉‥‥‥‥‥‥ 1杯
水‥‥‥‥‥‥ ½杯
沙拉油‥‥‥ 1大匙
塩、味精‥‥各少許
蛋‥‥‥‥‥‥ 1個

② 水‥‥‥‥‥‥ 1杯
白醋、糖‥‥各2大匙
番茄醬‥‥‥ 2大匙
塩‥‥‥‥‥‥ ⅛小匙

③ 水‥‥‥‥‥‥ 1大匙
太白粉‥‥‥ ⅔小匙

❶馬鈴薯、紅蘿蔔均去皮，入鍋煮熟，取出；馬鈴薯趁熱搗成泥，並將薯泥塞入荔枝內（圖一）；紅蘿蔔漂涼切滾刀塊，①料調成麵糊均備用。

❷炸油燒7分熱（約300°F），將荔枝沾麵糊入鍋炸成金黃色（圖二），撈起瀝油是爲元寶，備用。

❸鍋內留油少許，入青椒片、鳳梨片及紅蘿蔔拌炒數下，再入②料及元寶拌勻，最後以③料勾芡即成。

INGREDIENTS:

1 can		lychees
80 g (3 oz.)		potatoes
70 g (2½ oz.)		carrot
70 g (2½ oz.)		canned sliced pineapple (cut in pieces)
50 g (1¾ oz.)		green pepper pieces
6 c.		oil for frying
①	1 c.	flour
	½ c.	water
	1 T.	oil
	pinch	salt
	1	egg
②	1 c.	water
	2 T. each:	rice vinegar, ketchup, sugar
	⅛ t.	salt
③	1 T.	water
	⅔ t.	cornstarch

❶ Pare the potatoes and carrots and boil until soft. Remove from the water. Mash the potatoes while still hot. Stuff the mashed potatoes into the lychees (illus. 1). Cool the carrots in tap water and roll-cut. Mix ① into a smooth batter.

❷ Heat the oil to about 300°F (149°C). Dip the stuffed lychees in the batter and deep-fry until golden (illus. 2). Remove from the oil and drain. These are the "nuggets."

❸ Pour off all but a small amount of the oil. Stir-fry the green pepper, pineapple, and carrot briefly. Add ② and the "nuggets" and combine well. Thicken with ③ and serve.

6人份
SERVES 6

銀芽鱔糊

Vegetarian Eel in Sauce

材料：

銀芽·············	200公克	水················	½杯
紅蘿蔔絲·········	80公克	醬油、酒···各 1大匙	
厚香菇············	30公克	味精、糖···各½小匙	
芹菜段（ 3公分）·····	5段 ①	塩················	¼小匙
熟毛豆、薑絲···各 1大匙		水··············	1大匙
香菜末·············	1大匙	太白粉········	1小匙
炸油···············	3杯	麻油···········	2大匙

❶香菇泡軟去蒂切絲，炸油燒７分熱（300°Ｆ），炸香
香菇絲（圖一）撈起備用。

❷鍋內留油２大匙，爆香芹菜段，入紅蘿蔔絲，銀芽
拌炒數下，再入香菇絲，毛豆及①料拌炒數下盛盤
，上灑香菜末、薑絲，最後將麻油燒熱淋在薑絲上
（圖二）即成。

INGREDIENTS:

200 g (7 oz.)	mung bean sprouts (both ends removed)
80 g (3 oz.)	julienned carrots
30 g (1 oz.)	dried Chinese black mushrooms (thick)
5 pieces	Chinese celery (3 cm/1¾″ long)
1 T. each:	cooked fresh soybeans (or peas), shredded ginger root, minced fresh coriander
3 c.	oil for frying
½ c.	water
1 T. each:	soy sauce, rice wine
½ t. ①	sugar
¼ t.	salt
1 T.	water
1 t.	cornstarch
2 T.	sesame oil

❶ Soak the dried mushrooms until soft, remove the stems, and cut into julienne strips. Heat the oil for frying to about 300°F (149°C) and deep-fry the mushroom strips until fragrant (illus. 1). Remove from the oil and set aside.

❷ Pour off all but 2 tablespoons oil from the wok and fry the celery briefly. Add the carrot strips and bean sprouts and stir-fry briefly. Stir in the black mushroom strips, fresh soybeans, and ①, and stir-fry briefly again. Transfer to a serving plate and sprinkle on the minced fresh coriander and shredded ginger root. Finally, heat the sesame oil, pour over the shredded ginger root (illus. 2), and serve.

人份
SERVES 6

西芹吉條

Vegetarian Chicken With Celery

材料：

西芹	200公克		太白粉	2大匙
素鶏	100公克	①	味精、麻油	¼小匙
胡蘿蔔	80公克		塩、胡椒粉	少許
香菇	15公克		蛋	半個
紅辣椒絲	1大匙		水	½杯
薑末	½大匙	②	麻油	1大匙
炸油	4杯		塩、味精 各½小匙
			糖	½小匙
		③	水	1大匙
			太白粉	1小匙

❶ 西芹去老纖維，胡蘿蔔去皮，均切5公分長粗絲（圖一）；香菇泡軟去蒂（圖二）切絲，素鶏亦切粗絲入①料拌勻備用。

❷ 炸油燒7分熱，將❶料依序入油鍋過油再撈起瀝乾。

❸ 鍋內留油少許，爆香薑末及紅椒絲，再入所有過油之材料及②料拌炒數下，最後以③料勾芡即成。

INGREDIENTS:

200 g (7 oz.)		celery
100 g (3½ oz.)		vegetarian chicken chunks
80 g (3 oz.)		carrot
15 g (½ oz.)		dried Chinese black mushrooms
1 T.		shredded red chili pepper
½ T.		minced ginger root
4 c.		oil for frying
①	2 T.	cornstarch
	¼ t.	sesame oil
	pinch each:	salt, pepper
	½	egg
②	½ C.	water
	1 T.	sesame oil
	½ t. each:	salt, sugar
③	1 T.	water
	1 t.	cornstarch

❶ Remove some of the tough strings from the celery, and pare the carrot. Cut the celery and carrot into thick 5 cm (2″) long strips (illus. 1). Soak the dried mushrooms until soft, remove the stems (illus. 2), and cut into julienne strips. Cut the vegetarian chicken into thick strips and marinate in ①.

❷ Heat the oil to about 300°F (149°C) and deep-fry each of the ingredients in step ❶ separately for a very brief time. Drain.

❸ Pour off all but a small amount of the oil. Fry the minced ginger root and shredded red chili pepper briefly, then add the ingredients from step ❷ along with ②, stir-frying until well combined. Thicken with ③ and serve.

6人份
SERVES 6

雀巢若絲

Taro Nest with Pork Shreds

材料：

芋頭············	230公克	
銀芽············	120公克	①
胡蘿蔔絲········	50公克	
素肉············	30公克	
香菇絲··········	30公克	
芹菜············	8段	
薑絲············	1大匙	
炸油············	6杯	

① {
麵粉············ 2大匙
塩、味精···各½小匙
胡椒粉··········少許
}

② {
水············ 1½杯
味精、糖··各 1小匙
麻油············ 1小匙
塩············ ½小匙
胡椒粉··········少許
}

③ {
水············ ½大匙
太白粉········ ½小匙
}

❶芋頭去皮，刨成細絲，反覆泡水以洗去澱粉質（圖一），瀝乾後擦乾水份入①料拌勻，排入２個重疊的雀巢碗之中(圖二)，壓緊，炸油燒至８分熱(350°F)，將壓緊之芋頭炸黃取出即爲雀巢備用。

❷素肉泡溫水擠去水份切細絲備用。

❸鍋燒熱入油２大匙，爆香薑絲，即入芹菜段、香菇絲、胡蘿蔔絲、素肉絲、銀芽拌勻，再入②料炒熟，最後以③料勾芡盛起，放入雀巢中即成。

INGREDIENTS:

230 g (½ lb.)		taro (dasheen)
120 g (¼ lb.)		mung bean sprouts (with both ends removed)
50 g (1¾ oz.)		julienned carrot
30 g (1 oz.)		vegetarian pork
30 g (1 oz.)		dried Chinese black mushrooms, soaked until soft and julienned
8 pieces		celery
1 T.		shredded ginger root
6 c.		oil for frying

① {
2 T. — flour
½ t. — salt
pinch — pepper
}

② {
1½ c. — water
1 t. each: — sugar, sesame oil
½ t. — salt
pinch — pepper
}

③ {
½ T. — water
½ t. — cornstarch
}

❶ Peel the taros, shred, and rinse repeatedly to remove the starchy coating (illus. 1). Drain well, pat dry with paper towels, and mix with ① . Form into a nest between two bowls as shown (illus. 2). Press down hard to make the nest hold its shape. Heat the oil to about 350°F (177°C) and fry the taro nest until golden.

❷ Soak the vegetarian pork in warm water until soft. Squeeze out the excess moisture and cut into julienne strips.

❸ Heat a wok and add 2 tablespoons oil. Fry the shredded ginger root, then add the celery, mushroom strips, carrot strips, vegetarian pork strips, and the bean sprouts, mixing thoroughly. Add ② and stir-fry until the ingredients are cooked through, then thicken with ③. Pour into the taro nest and serve.

6人份
SERVES 6

沙茶素寶

Pork Slices With Barbecue Sauce

材料：

素肉片	50公克
芥藍菜	300公克
芹菜末、薑末	各 1大匙
紅辣椒末	1大匙
油	2杯

① {
蛋	1個
太白粉	4小匙
味精	½小匙
塩	¼小匙
胡椒粉	少許

② {
水	1杯
素沙茶醬	2大匙
醬油、麻油	1大匙
味精	1小匙

③ {
太白粉	1小匙
水	1大匙

❶ 將芥藍菜頭尾修齊（圖一），留約10公分長，以熱水6杯加油2大匙，燙熟撈起瀝乾排盤備用。

❷ 素肉片泡溫水，擠乾水份（圖二），入①料拌勻，油2杯燒熱，將素肉片過油備用。

❸ 鍋內留油2大匙，爆香芹菜末、薑末、紅辣椒末，入素肉片及②料拌炒均勻，再以③料勾芡盛起淋在芥藍菜上即成。

INGREDIENTS:

50 g (1¾ oz.)	vegetarian pork slices
300 g (⅔ lb.)	Chinese kale (kailan choi)
1 T. each:	minced Chinese celery, minced ginger root, minced red chili pepper
2 c.	oil

① {
1	egg
4 t.	cornstarch
¼ t.	salt
pinch	pepper

② {
1 c.	water
2 T.	vegetarian Chinese barbecue sauce (su sha cha chiang)
1 T. each:	soy sauce, sesame oil

③ {
1 t.	cornstarch
1 T.	water

❶ Trim both ends of the Chinese kale (illus. 1) so that all the stalks measure about 10 cm (4″) long. Cook until just done in 6 cups of water and 2 tablespoons oil. Remove, drain, and place on a plate.

❷ Soak the vegetarian pork slices in warm water until soft. Squeeze out the excess moisture (illus. 2) and mix in ①. Heat 2 cups of oil, and deep-fry the vegetarian pork slices briefly.

❸ Pour off all but 2 tablespoons of the oil. Fry the minced Chinese celery, minced ginger root, and minced red chili pepper. Add the vegetarian pork slices and ② and stir-fry until well combined. Thicken with ③, and pour over the Chinese kale. Serve.

6人份
SERVES 6

京醬若絲

Peking Style Pork Shreds

材料：

麵腸	250公克	水	1杯
小黃瓜	200公克	甜麵醬	2大匙
芹菜末	1大匙	麻油、糖…各	1大匙
油	2杯	② 番茄醬	1小匙
		醬油	1小匙
① 蛋	半個	味精	½小匙
油	1大匙	胡椒粉	少許
麻油	1小匙	③ 太白粉	2小匙
太白粉	1小匙	水	2大匙
味精	½小匙		
塩	¼小匙		

❶小黃瓜切絲泡冷水約5分鐘撈起，瀝乾水份排盤備用。

❷麵腸切絲(圖一)，入①料拌勻(圖二)；油2杯燒6分熱(250°F)，麵腸過油備用。

❸鍋內留油2大匙，爆香芹菜末，即入麵腸及②料炒熟，再以③料勾芡即成。

INGREDIENTS:

250 g (9 oz.)		vegetarian (wheat gluten) sausage
200 g (7 oz.)		gherkin cucumbers
1 T.		minced Chinese celery
2 c.		oil
①	½	egg
	1 T.	oil
	1 t. each:	sesame oil, cornstarch
	¼ t.	salt
②	1 c.	water
	2 T.	sweet bean paste
	1 t. each:	sesame oil, sugar
	1 t. each:	ketchup, soy sauce
	pinch	pepper
③	2 t.	cornstarch
	2 T.	water

❶ Cut the gherkin cucumber into julienne strips. Soak in cold water about 5 minutes and remove. Drain well and place on a plate.

❷ Cut the vegetarian sausage into julienne strips (illus. 1) and marinate in ① (illus. 2). Heat 2 cups oil to about 250°F (121°C). Deep-fry the vegetarian sausage strips briefly.

❸ Pour off all but 2 tablespoons of the oil. Fry the minced Chinese celery briefly, then add the vegetarian sausage strips and ② and stir-fry until cooked through. Thicken with ③ and serve.

6人份
SERVES 6

糖醋子排

Sweet and Sour Ribs

材料：

油條………………………	1條		水………………	1杯
芋頭(淨重)……	60公克	②	番茄醬………	2大匙
紅蘿蔔片…………	50公克		糖、白醋…各	2小匙
青椒片…………	50公克		塩………………	¼小匙
罐頭鳳梨片……	50公克	③	水……………	1大匙
┌麵粉…………	1杯		太白粉………	⅔小匙
│水 …………	⅓杯		炸油…………	6杯
①│沙拉油………	1大匙			
│塩、味精……	¼小匙			
└蛋……………	1個			

❶ ①料調成麵糊備用。

❷ 將油條1條剝成兩小條，每條再切5公分長段，芋頭切0.5×5公分長條(圖一)，塞入油條中(圖二)備用。

❸ 炸油燒6分熱(約250°F)，將❷料沾麵糊入鍋炸成金黃色，撈起瀝油，是爲素排骨。

❹ 鍋內留油少許，入紅蘿蔔片、青椒片、鳳梨片拌炒數下，即入②料煮沸並以③料勾芡，後入素排骨拌勻即成。

INGREDIENTS:

	1	Chinese fried cruller (you-tiao)
	60 g (2 oz.)	taro (net wt.)
	50 g (1¾ oz.)	carrot slices
	50 g (1¾ oz.)	green pepper pieces
	50 g (1¾ oz.)	canned sliced pineapple, cut into pieces
①	⎧ 1 c.	flour
	⎪ ⅓ c.	water
	⎨ 1 T.	oil
	⎪ ¼ t.	salt
	⎩ 1	egg
②	⎧ 1 c.	water
	⎪ 2 T.	ketchup
	⎨ 2 t. each:	sugar, rice vinegar
	⎩ ¼ t.	salt
③	⎧ 1 T.	water
	⎨ ⅔ t.	cornstarch
	6 c.	oil for frying

❶ Mix ① into a smooth batter.

❷ Separate the two halves of the Chinese fried cruller lengthwise, then cut each half into 5 cm (2″) pieces. Cut the taro into 5×0.5 cm (2″×¼″) strips (illus. 1). Stuff inside the pieces of fried cruller (illus. 2).

❸ Heat the oil to about 250°F (121°C). Dip the stuffed crullers into the batter and deep-fry until golden. Remove from the oil and drain. These are the vegetarian ''ribs.''

❹ Pour off all but a small amount of oil from the wok, then stir-fry the carrot slices, green pepper pieces, and pineapple pieces briefly. Add ② and bring to a boil. Thicken with ③, mix in the vegetarian ribs until well coated, and serve.

6人份
SERVES 6

腰果芋球

Taro Croquettes With Cashews

材料：

芋頭	300公克
罐頭鳳梨丁	70公克
紅蘿蔔丁	50公克
青椒丁	30公克
乾木耳	10公克
炸好之腰果	½杯
炸油	6杯

① { 糖 ½杯
　　麵粉 3大匙 }

② { 水 ½杯
　　番茄醬 1½大匙
　　糖 1½大匙
　　白醋 1小匙
　　塩 少許 }

③ { 水 ½大匙
　　太白粉 ½小匙 }

❶木耳泡軟去蒂（圖一），切成小丁備用。

❷芋頭去皮，切片，蒸熟，壓成泥，與①料拌勻再分成18等份，每份捏成橄欖形之芋球（圖二）；炸油燒7分熱（約300°F）將芋球炸成金黃色撈起備用。

❸鍋熱入油2大匙，將青椒丁、紅蘿蔔丁、鳳梨丁和木耳丁炒8分熟，即入②料燒開，再以③料勾芡，起鍋前入芋球及腰果拌勻即成。

6人份
SERVES 6

INGREDIENTS:

300 g (⅔ lb.)	taro
70 g (2½ oz.)	canned pineapple cubes
50 g (1¾ oz.)	carrot cubes
30 g (1 oz.)	green pepper cubes
10 g (⅓ oz.)	dried wood ears (mu erh)
½ c.	deep-fried cashews
6 c.	oil for frying

① { ⅓ c. — sugar
　　3 T. — flour }

② { ½ c. — water
　　1½ T. — ketchup
　　1½ T. — sugar
　　1 t. — rice vinegar
　　pinch — salt }

③ { ½ T. — water
　　½ t. — cornstarch }

❶ Soak the wood ears until soft and remove the tough stem portion (illus. 1). Dice.

❷ Pare the taro, slice, and steam until soft. Mash and mix well with ①. Divide into 18 equal portions, then form each one into an olive shape (illus. 2). Heat the oil to about 300°F (149°C) and fry the taro croquettes until golden. Remove from the oil.

❸ Heat a wok and add 2 tablespoons oil. Stir-fry the green pepper, carrots, pineapple, and wood ears until about half done. Mix in ② and bring to a boil. Thicken with ③, stir in the taro croquettes and cashews until well coated, and serve.

魚香茄餅

Eggplant Fritters in Sauce

材料：

茄子⋯⋯⋯⋯⋯ 150公克		辣豆瓣醬⋯⋯⋯⋯ 1大匙	
素烏魚子⋯⋯⋯⋯80公克		② 水⋯⋯⋯⋯⋯⋯ 1杯	

薑末
荸薺末　各 1大匙
玉米筍末
芹菜末

② 醬油⋯⋯⋯⋯ 2小匙
酒釀⋯⋯⋯⋯ 1小匙
麻油⋯⋯⋯⋯ 1小匙
白醋⋯⋯⋯⋯ 1小匙
糖、味精⋯各½小匙
塩⋯⋯⋯⋯⋯⅛小匙

① 麵粉⋯⋯⋯⋯ 1杯
水⋯⋯⋯⋯⋯ ½杯
沙拉油⋯⋯⋯ 1大匙
塩、味精⋯⋯¼小匙
蛋⋯⋯⋯⋯⋯ 1個

③ 水⋯⋯⋯⋯⋯ 1大匙
太白粉⋯⋯⋯⅔小匙

❶ ①料拌勻調成麵糊，素烏魚子切 3×2.5×0.5 公分片狀備用。

❷ 茄子洗淨去頭，每隔0.5公分寬切斜片，第一刀勿斷（圖一），第二刀再切斷（圖二），再將每片素烏魚子夾在每片茄子中央（圖三）備用。

❸ 炸油燒7分熱（約300° F），將茄餅沾麵糊，入鍋炸成金黃色撈起瀝油備用。

❹ 鍋內留油少許，入薑末、荸薺末、玉米筍末及辣豆瓣醬爆香，再入②料拌炒數下，待煮沸時以③料勾芡，再續入茄餅拌勻，起鍋前灑上芹菜末即成。

INGREDIENTS:

150 g (⅓ lb.)		Oriental eggplant
80 g (3 oz.)		vegetarian fish roe
1 T. each:		minced ginger root, minced water chestnuts, minced baby corn, minced Chinese celery

①
1 c. flour
½ c. water
1 T. oil
¼ t. salt
1 egg

1 T. hot bean paste

②
1 c. water
2 t. soy sauce
1 t. each: sweet fermented rice, sesame oil, rice vinegar
½ t. sugar
⅛ t. salt

③
1 T. water
⅔ t. cornstarch

❶ Mix ① into a smooth batter. Cut the vegetarian fish roe into 3×2.5×0.5 cm (1¼″ × 1″ × ¼″) slices.

❷ Wash the Oriental eggplant and cut off the ends. Make slashes at 0.5 cm (¼″) intervals; cut all the way through *only* on alternate cuts (illus. 1, 2). Sandwich a slice of vegetarian fish roe inside each split piece of eggplant (illus. 3).

❸ Heat the oil for frying to about 300°F (149°C). Dip each piece of stuffed eggplant into the batter and deep-fry until golden. Remove from the oil and drain.

❹ Pour off all but a small amount of the oil. Fry the minced ginger root, minced water chestnuts, minced baby corn, and hot bean paste briefly. Add ② and continue to stir-fry until the mixture comes to a boil. Thicken with ③, then add the eggplant fritters and mix to coat. Sprinkle the minced Chinese celery over the top and serve.

干燒明蝦

Prawns in Tomato Sauce

材料：

豆腐皮················ 3張	
馬鈴薯········· 200公克	
胡蘿蔔········· 100公克	
蛋白················ ½個	
薑末··············· 1大匙	
紅辣椒末·········· 1小匙	
芹菜末············· 1大匙	
炸油················ 6杯	

① { 塩、味精···各¼小匙 / 胡椒粉········¼小匙

② {
蛋················ 1個
水················ 1杯
麵粉·············· ¾杯
油··············· 2大匙
塩、味精······ ½小匙

③ {
水··············· 1½杯
番茄醬············ 2大匙
酒釀············ 2大匙
辣椒醬············ 1大匙
麻油············· 1大匙
糖、味精·········· 1小匙
塩·············· ½小匙
胡椒粉·········· 少許
白醋·············· 1小匙

④ {
水················ 1大匙
太白粉········· 1小匙

❶ 胡蘿蔔、馬鈴薯煮熟去皮壓成泥(圖一)，入①料拌匀成餡，分成9等份備用。

❷ 每張豆腐皮切成3等份，1張豆腐皮取餡1份(圖二)，以蛋白封口包成蝦形(圖三)，再以大火蒸5分鐘取出待涼，即爲素明蝦。

❸ ②料拌匀是爲麵糊，炸油燒熱，素明蝦沾上麵糊炸黃撈起瀝油排盤。

❹ 鍋內留油2大匙，爆香薑末、紅辣椒末後，入③料煮開以④料勾芡，淋在素明蝦上，最後灑上芹菜末即可。

INGREDIENTS:

3 sheets	bean curd skin
200 g (7 oz.)	potatoes
100 g (3½ oz.)	carrot
½	egg white
1 T.	minced ginger root
1 t.	minced red chili pepper
1 T.	minced Chinese celery
6 c.	oil for frying

① ¼ t. each: salt, pepper

② {
1 egg
1 c. water
¾ c. flour
2 T. oil
½ t. salt

③ {
1½ c. water
2 T. each: ketchup, sweet fermented rice
1 T. each: chili paste, sesame oil
1 t. each: sugar, rice vinegar
½ t. salt
pinch pepper

④ {
1 T. water
1 t. cornstarch

❶ Pare the carrot and potatoes, cook until soft, and mash until smooth (illus. 1). Mix in ① to make a filling. Divide it into 9 equal portions.

❷ Cut each sheet of bean curd skin into 3 equal portions. Wrap a portion of filling (illus. 2) in each piece of bean curd skin. Seal shut tightly with egg white while forming it into the shape of a large shrimp (illus. 3). Steam 5 minutes over high heat. Remove from the steamer and allow to cool. These are the vegetarian "prawns."

❸ Mix ② to form a smooth batter. Heat the oil for frying, dip the vegetarian prawns into the batter, and deep-fry until golden. Remove from the oil, drain, and arrange on a serving platter.

❹ Pour off all but 2 tablespoons oil from the wok. Fry the minced ginger root and minced red chili pepper briefly, then add ③ and bring to a boil. Thicken with ④, pour over the prawns, and sprinkle a little minced Chinese celery over the top. Serve.

❶

❷

❸

扁尖腐衣

Bean Curd Skin with Bamboo Shoots

材料：

熟毛豆	……………80公克
扁尖	……………20公克
豆腐皮	…………… 8張
油	…………… 2大匙

①
水	…………… 1杯
醬油	………… 2小匙
味精	………… ½小匙
麻油、塩	………少許

❶ 扁尖泡軟剪0.5×4公分（圖一），豆腐皮泡水捏乾水
　份切成4×2公分（圖二）備用。

❷ 鍋熱入油2大匙，再入扁尖及①料煮約5分鐘，續
　入豆腐皮及毛豆續煮至水略收乾即成。

INGREDIENTS:

80 g (3 oz.)	cooked fresh soybeans
20 g (¾ oz.)	dried bamboo shoots
8 sheets	bean curd skin
2 T.	oil

①
1 c.	water
2 t.	soy sauce
dash	sesame oil
pinch	salt

❶ Soak the dried bamboo shoots in water until
soft. With a scissors, cut into 0.5×4 cm (¼" ×
1½") strips (illus. 1). Soak the bean curd skin
briefly in water, squeeze out the excess
moisture, and cut into 4×2 cm (1½"×1½")
squares (illus. 2).

❷ Heat a wok and add 2 tablespoons oil. Add
the bamboo shoots and ①, bring to a boil,
and allow to cook about 5 minutes. Add the
bean curd skin and cooked fresh soybeans,
and continue cooking until the liquid is
reduced. Serve.

6人份
SERVES 6

油燜黃雀

Braised Vegetarian Partridge

材料：

芥菜	80公克
豆干	50公克
香菇	15公克
豆皮	4張
炸油	6杯

① { 麻油 …… 1小匙 / 塩、味精 …… 各少許 / 糖 …… 少許 }

② { 水 …… 1杯 / 醬油 …… 2小匙 / 味精 …… ½小匙 }

③ { 水 …… 1大匙 / 太白粉 …… ½小匙 / 胡椒粉 …… 少許 }

❶香菇泡軟去蒂切末，豆干與芥菜亦切末，入①料拌勻成餡分成8等份備用。

❷豆皮4張對切成8張（圖一），每小張豆皮包1份餡，捲起來再打結（圖二）是為黃雀，共8份備用。

❸炸油燒8分熱（約350°F），將黃雀炸成金黃色撈起瀝油。②料與炸好之黃雀一起燜煮5分鐘，入③料勾茨即成。

INGREDIENTS:

80 g (3 oz.)	fresh mustard greens
50 g (1¾ oz.)	pressed bean curd (*tou kan*)
15 g (½ oz.)	dried Chinese black mushrooms
4 sheets	bean curd skin
6 c.	oil for frying

① { 1 t. / pinch each: } { sesame oil / salt, sugar }

② { 1 c. / 2 t. } { water / soy sauce }

③ { 1 T. / ½ t. / pinch } { water / cornstarch / pepper }

❶ Soak the dried mushrooms until soft, remove the stems, and mince. Mince the pressed bean curd and mustard greens. Mix in ① to make a filling. Divide into 8 equal portions.

❷ Cut the 4 sheets of bean curd skin in half, making 8 pieces (illus. 1). Wrap one portion of filling in each piece of bean curd skin, rolling it up and tying it (illus. 2). These are the "partridges."

❸ Heat the oil to about 350°F (177°C), and deep-fry the "partridges" until golden. Remove from the oil and drain. Braise the "partridges" in ②, covered and over low heat, about 5 minutes. Thicken with ③ and serve.

6人份
SERVES 6

脆鱔　　　Crispy Eel

材料：

大花菇…………40公克		水……………2大匙
太白粉…………4大匙	②	太白粉………2小匙
炸油……………4杯		麻油…………少許

①{
水……………1杯
糖……………4大匙
薑汁………1小匙
醋…………½小匙
五香粉………少許
}

❶大花菇泡軟去蒂，依菇傘形剪成1.5 公分寬的長條
　形（圖一），擠去水份再沾太白粉（圖二）備用。
❷油燒７分熱（約300°Ｆ），將花菇條入鍋炸脆撈起。
❸鍋內留油２大匙，入①料煮沸，再以②料勾芡後，
　倒入炸過之花菇拌炒數下即成。

INGREDIENTS:

40 g (1½ oz.)	large dried Chinese black mushrooms
4 T.	cornstarch
4 c.	oil for frying

①{
1 c.　　　　water
4 T.　　　　sugar
1 t.　　　　ginger root juice
½ t.　　　　rice vinegar
pinch　　　Chinese five-spice powder
}

②{
2 T.　　　　water
2 t.　　　　cornstarch
dash　　　　sesame oil
}

❶ Soak the large dried Chinese black mushrooms until
soft and remove the stems. Cut 1.5 cm (⅔″) wide
strips from the mushrooms by cutting around the
outside edge (illus. 1). Squeeze out the excess
moisture, dredge in cornstarch (illus. 2), and set
aside.

❷ Heat the oil to about 300°F (149°C). Deep-fry the
mushroom strips until crisp, and remove from the oil.

❸ Pour off all but 2 tablespoons of the oil, add ①, and
bring to a boil. Thicken with ②. Add the deep-fried
mushroom strips, stir to coat with the sauce, and
serve.

6人份
SERVES 6

紅燒麵結

Stuffed Bean Curd Sheets

材料：

百頁	6張	① {	温水 3杯
高麗菜	100公克		鹼塊 ¼小塊
金菇	80公克	② {	水 4杯
綠竹筍片	50公克		塩 1大匙
紅蘿蔔片	50公克	③ {	塩、味精 各少許
草菇片	50公克		胡椒粉 少許
香菇	15公克	④ {	水 1杯
熟毛豆	15公克		醬油 2小匙
油	2大匙		味精 ½小匙
太白粉	1小匙		麻油 少許

❶ 百頁攤開入①料泡約6分鐘，再以②料將鹼味洗淨。
❷ 香菇泡軟去蒂與高麗菜均切絲，金菇洗淨去頭備用。
❸ 鍋熱入油1大匙，將❷炒熟入③料拌勻，取出瀝乾（圖一），再入太白粉拌勻成餡，分成6等份，1張百頁包1份餡，捲成6公分的長捲（圖二），入蒸籠蒸15分鐘，取出是為麵結。
❹ 鍋熱入油1大匙，將筍片、紅蘿蔔片、草菇片炒熟，續入④料與麵結再煮5分鐘，起鍋前灑上熟毛豆即成。

6人份
SERVES 6

INGREDIENTS:

6	bean curd sheets (*pai yeh*)
100 g (3½ oz.)	cabbage
80 g (3 oz.)	*enoki* (golden mushrooms)
50 g (1¾ oz.)	sliced bamboo shoots
50 g (1¾ oz.)	sliced carrots
50 g (1¾ oz.)	sliced straw mushrooms
15 g (½ oz.)	dried Chinese black mushrooms
15 g (½ oz.)	cooked fresh soybeans (or peas)
2 T.	oil
1 t.	cornstarch
① { 3 c.	warm water
1 t.	baking soda
② { 4 c.	water
1 T.	salt
③ pinch each:	salt, pepper
④ { 1 c.	water
2 t.	soy sauce
dash	sesame oil

❶ Spread open the bean curd sheets (*pai yeh*) and soak in ① about 6 minutes. Drain, and remove the soda flavor with ②.
❷ Soak the dried mushrooms until soft and remove the stems. Cut the mushrooms and cabbage into shreds. Wash the *enoki*, trim off the tough ends, and set aside.
❸ Heat a wok and add 1 tablespoon oil. Stir-fry the ingredients from step ❷ until done, then stir in ③. Remove and drain (illus. 1). Mix in the cornstarch to make a filling, and divide into 6 equal portions. Wrap one portion of filling in each bean curd sheet, rolling it up into a 6 cm (2½") cylinder (illus. 2). Steam 15 minutes. Remove from steamer.
❹ Heat a wok and add 1 tablespoon oil. Stir-fry the sliced bamboo shoots, sliced carrot, and sliced straw mushrooms until just done. Add ④ and the stuffed bean curd sheets, and cook 5 minutes. Sprinkle the cooked fresh soybeans over the top before transferring to a serving dish.

乾燒筍

Soy-Simmered Bamboo Shoots

材料：

筍·················· 600公克	
荸薺末··············80公克	
玉米筍末··········70公克	
薑末··············· ½大匙	
炸油················· 4杯	
辣豆瓣醬··········· 1大匙	

① {
水··············· ½杯
醬油········ 1½小匙
酒釀、香油··· 1小匙
糖、白醋··各 ½小匙
塩、味精··· ⅛小匙
}

② {
水············· ½大匙
太白粉········ ½小匙
麻油·········· ¼小匙
}

❶ 筍去殼切滾刀塊（圖一），炸油燒７分熱（約300°Ｆ）
　，將筍炸至金黃色（圖二）撈起瀝油備用。
❷ 鍋內留油少許入薑末、玉米筍末、荸薺末及辣豆瓣
　醬爆香，再入①料煮沸，續入筍以小火燒煮５分鐘
　，後入②料勾芡即成。

INGREDIENTS:

600 g (1⅓ lb.)		bamboo shoots
80 g (3 oz.)		minced water chestnuts
70 g (2½ oz.)		minced baby corn
½ T.		minced ginger root
4 c.		oil for frying
1 T.		hot bean paste
①	½ c.	water
	1½ t.	soy sauce
	1 t. each:	sweet fermented rice, sesame oil
	½ t. each:	sugar, rice vinegar
	⅛ t.	salt
②	½ T.	water
	½ t.	cornstarch
	¼ t.	sesame oil

❶ Husk the bamboo shoots and roll-cut (illus. 1).
　Heat the oil for frying to about 300°F (149°C).
　Deep-fry the bamboo shoots until golden (illus.
　2), remove from the oil, and drain.
❷ Pour off all but a small amount of oil. Fry the
　minced ginger root, minced baby corn,
　minced water chestnuts, and hot bean paste
　briefly. Add ① and bring to a boil. Add the
　bamboo shoots and cook 5 minutes over low
　heat. Thicken with ② and serve.

6人份
SERVES 6

豆瓣錦鯉

Carp in Bean Paste

材料：

素魚‥‥‥‥‥‥ 1條		糖、味精‥‥各½小匙		
荸薺末 ⎫		水‥‥‥‥‥‥ 1½杯		
玉米筍末 ⎬ ‥‥‥各1大匙		醬油‥‥‥‥‥ 2小匙		
薑末 ⎭	①	酒釀‥‥‥‥‥ 1小匙		
炸油‥‥‥‥‥‥ 4杯		麻油‥‥‥‥‥ 1小匙		
辣豆瓣醬‥‥‥‥ 1大匙		白醋‥‥‥‥‥ 1小匙		
		塩‥‥‥‥‥‥ ⅛小匙		
	②	水‥‥‥‥‥‥ 1大匙		
		太白粉‥‥‥‥ ⅔小匙		

❶將素魚切交叉斜線花紋，炸油燒8分熱（約350°Ｆ）
，入鍋炸成金黃色（圖一），撈起瀝油備用。

❷鍋內留油少許，入薑末、玉米筍末、荸薺末及辣豆
瓣醬爆香，再入①料（圖二），待煮沸後入炸好的素
魚煮約3分鐘，取出素魚排盤，餘汁以②料勾茨淋
在素魚上即成。

INGREDIENTS:

1		whole vegetarian fish
1 T. each:		minced water chestnuts, minced baby corn, minced ginger root
4 c.		oil for frying
1 T.		hot bean paste
	½ t. each:	sugar
	1½ c.	water
①	2 t.	soy sauce
	1 t. each:	sweet fermented rice, sesame oil, rice vinegar
	⅛ t.	salt
②	1 T.	water
	⅔ t.	cornstarch

❶ Make a series of diagonal slashes in the vegetarian
fish. Heat the oil to about 350°F (177°C). Deep-fry the
fish until golden (illus. 1), remove from the oil, and
drain.

❷ Pour off all but a small amount of the oil. Fry the
minced ginger root, minced baby corn, minced
water chestnut, and hot bean paste briefly. Add ①
(illus. 2) and bring to a boil . Add the fried vegetarian
fish and continue to cook about 3 minutes. Remove
the fish and place on a serving platter. Thicken the
remaining liquid with ② while continuing to heat.
Drizzle the sauce over the vegetarian fish and serve.

6人份
SERVES 6

枇杷豆腐

材料：

嫩豆腐	1塊
紅蘿蔔	50公克
荸薺	50公克
青豆仁	50公克
炸油	6杯
蛋白	2個

①
玉米粉	1½大匙
味精	½小匙
塩	¼小匙
胡椒粉	少許
蛋	1個

②
水	1½杯
麻油	½大匙
塩、味精	各¼小匙
胡椒粉	少許

③
水	1大匙
太白粉	⅔小匙

❶ 紅蘿蔔去皮切3公分直徑的半圓形薄片，荸薺切0.3公分寬的圓片，青豆洗淨備用。

❷ 豆腐洗淨以毛巾吸乾水份，入①料以打蛋器攪拌成豆腐泥，分成12等份備用。

❸ 炸油燒6分熱（約250°F）後關小火，將每份豆腐泥捏成枇杷狀（圖一），共捏12個，炸成金黃色（圖二）撈起瀝油備用。

❹ 鍋內留油少許，續入紅蘿蔔片、荸薺片、青豆仁爆炒數下，再入②料煮沸，續入枇杷以小火燒約3分鐘後，以③料勾芡，起鍋前淋下蛋白，待蛋白熟後拌匀即成。

Loquat Bean Curd

INGREDIENTS:

1 large cake	soft bean curd (tofu)
50 g (1¾ oz.)	carrot
50 g (1¾ oz.)	water chestnuts
50 g (1¾ oz.)	peas
6 c.	oil for frying
2	egg whites

①
1½ T.	cornstarch
¼ t.	salt
pinch	pepper
1	egg

②
1½ c.	water
½ T.	sesame oil
¼ t.	salt
pinch	pepper

③
1 T.	water
⅔ t.	cornstarch

❶ Pare the carrots and cut into thin semi-circles with a radius of about 3 cm (1¼"). Cut the water chestnuts into 0.3 cm (⅛") thick rounds. Wash the peas.

❷ Wash the bean curd, then wrap in a white cloth and gently squeeze out as much moisture as possible. Add ① and mash well with an egg whisk. Divide into 12 equally-sized portions.

❸ Heat the oil to about 250°F (121°C), then lower the heat. Form each portion of mashed bean curd into the shape of a loquat (or long plum; illus. 1). Deep-fry until golden (illus. 2), remove from the oil, and drain.

❹ Pour off all but a small amount of the oil. Fry the carrot, water chestnuts, and peas briefly. Add ② and bring to a boil. Add the "loquat bean curd" balls, and cook 3 minutes in the sauce over low heat. Thicken with ③. Drizzle the egg whites over the top before transferring to a serving dish. When the egg whites are set, mix together and serve.

6人份
SERVES 6

菜心獅子頭

Lion's Head With Greens

材料：

老豆腐	1塊		
青江菜	300公克	② 太白粉	1½大匙
梅干菜	60公克	糖、鹽	各⅛小匙
炸油	6杯	蛋白	1個
① 素高湯	1杯	③ 素高湯	2杯
醬油	1大匙	醬油	1大匙
糖	1小匙	糖、味精	½小匙
		麻油、鹽	各少許
		④ 水	1大匙
		太白粉	⅔小匙

INGREDIENTS:

1 large cake		firm bean curd (tofu)
300 g (⅔ lb.)		ching kang tsai (or other leafy green)
60 g (2 oz.)		dried mustard greens (mei kan tsai)
6 c.		oil for frying
①	1 c.	vegetarian stock
	1 T.	soy sauce
	1 t.	sugar
②	1½ T.	cornstarch
	⅛ t. each:	sugar, salt
	1	egg white
③	2 c.	vegetarian stock
	1 T.	soy sauce
	½ t.	sugar
	dash	sesame oil
	pinch	salt
④	1 T.	water
	⅔ t.	cornstarch

❶ 青江菜、豆腐洗淨，並以白布包起豆腐擠乾水份備用；梅干菜洗淨切末（圖一），與①料以小火燜煮10分鐘，取出擠乾水份再與豆腐拌勻成餡均分四等份，每份捏成圓球狀（圖二）是為素獅子頭備用。

❷ 炸油燒5分熱（約200°F），將素獅子頭入鍋炸至金黃色撈起瀝油備用。

❸ 鍋內留油少許，將青江菜略炒，入③料與獅子頭再以中火續煮約10分鐘後入④料勾芡即成。

❶ Wash the greens and the bean curd. Wrap the bean curd in a clean white cloth and gently squeeze out as much moisture as possible. Wash the dried mustard greens thoroughly and mince (illus. 1). Simmer 10 minutes in ①, covered, over low heat. Remove and squeeze out the excess moisture. Mash together with the bean curd and divide into 4 equal portions, forming each into a ball. This is vegetarian ''lion's head.''

❷ Heat the oil to about 200°F (93°C) and deep-fry the lion's heads until golden. Remove from the oil and drain.

❸ Pour off all but a small amount of the oil. Stir-fry the greens briefly, then add ③ and the lion's heads. Cook about 10 minutes over medium heat. Thicken with ④ and serve.

6人份
SERVES 6

紅燒烤麩

Soy-Simmered Bran Puffs

材料：

冬筍	300公克		水	2杯
烤麩	120公克		醬油	4大匙
紅蘿蔔	80公克	①	麻油	1大匙
豆干	70公克		薑汁	1大匙
厚香菇(小朶)	10公克		糖	⅔大匙
炸油	6杯			

❶ 烤麩切3×3×0.5公分片(圖一)，炸油燒7分熱(約300°F)，將烤麩炸成金黃色(圖二)撈起瀝油備用。

❷ 冬筍去殼切3×2×0.5公分片狀，紅蘿蔔去皮亦切同大小片狀，香菇泡軟去蒂，豆干每塊等切成4小塊備用。

❸ 筍片、紅蘿蔔片、豆干、香菇與①料同入鍋，以中火燒10分鐘，後入烤麩，以小火續燒數分鐘，待湯汁快收乾即成。

INGREDIENTS:

300 g (⅔ lb.)	bamboo shoots
120 g (¼ lb.)	bran puffs (kao fu)
80 g (3 oz.)	carrot
70 g (2½ oz.)	pressed bean curd (tou kan)
10 g (⅓ oz.)	small, thick dried Chinese black mushrooms
6 c.	oil for frying
① { 2 c.	water
4 T.	soy sauce
1 T. each:	sesame oil, ginger root juice
⅔ T.	sugar

❶ Cut the bran puffs into 3×3×0.5 cm (1¼″ × 1¼″ × ¼″) slices (illus. 1). Heat the oil to about 300°F (149°C) and deep-fry the bran puffs until golden (illus. 2). Remove from the oil and drain.

❷ Husk the bamboo shoots and cut into 3×2×0.5 cm (1¼″ × ¾″ × ¼″) slices. Pare the carrot and cut into slices about the same size as the bamboo shoots. Soak the dried mushrooms until soft and remove the stems. Cut each piece of pressed bean curd into 4 small pieces.

❸ Place the sliced bamboo shoots, sliced carrots, pressed bean curd, and ① in a wok and cook 10 minutes over medium heat. Last add the bran puffs and cook another several minutes over low heat until the liquid is reduced. Serve.

6 人份
SERVES 6

紅燒元菜

Soy-Simmered Tortoise

材料：

大香菇……12朵（約40克）		水……………… 1杯
金針……18根（約20公克）		醬油……… 1½大匙
筍………………60公克		糖、酒……各 1大匙
胡蘿蔔……………60公克	①	麻油………… 1大匙
豌豆片……………10公克		番茄醬……… 1小匙
芹菜末、薑末…各 1大匙		味精……………少許
炸油………………… 3杯		胡椒粉…………少許
	②	水……… 1½大匙
		太白粉…… 1½小匙

❶ 香菇泡軟去蒂擠乾水份，金針泡軟去頭，筍和紅蘿蔔煮熟切滾刀塊，豌豆片去老梗燙熟備用。

❷ 每朵香菇內面均沾太白粉（圖一），每2片香菇中間排入金針呈"＊"狀後壓扁（圖二），即為元菜，共有6個，以大火蒸10分鐘取出放涼，炸油燒熱，元菜稍炸撈起備用。

❸ 鍋內留油2大匙，爆香芹菜末、薑末，再入①料煮開，續入元菜、筍、胡蘿蔔塊燜煮5分鐘，後入②料勾芡，起鍋前倒入豌豆片及熱油1大匙即成。

INGREDIENTS:

12	large dried Chinese black mushrooms (about 40 g or 1½ oz.)
18	dried lily buds (about 20 g or ⅔ oz.)
60 g (2 oz.)	bamboo shoots
60 g (2 oz.)	carrots
10 g (⅓ oz.)	Chinese peapods
1 T. each:	minced Chinese celery, minced ginger root
3 c.	oil for frying
	1 c.	water
	1½ T.	soy sauce
①	1 T. each:	sugar, rice wine, sesame oil
	1 t.	ketchup
	pinch	pepper
②	1½ T.	water
	1½ t.	cornstarch

❶ Soak the dried mushrooms until soft, remove the stems, and squeeze out the excess moisture. Soak the dried lily buds until soft and trim off the tough ends. Boil the bamboo shoots and carrots until soft and roll-cut. Snap the ends and remove the strings from the Chinese peapods. Blanch briefly in boiling water.

❷ Dredge the inside of each mushroom in cornstarch (illus. 1). Fit three lily buds inside 6 of the mushroom caps into the shape of a ＊ , then press another mushroom on top of each (illus. 2) to make the vegetarian "tortoises". Steam 10 minutes over high heat. Remove from the steamer and allow to cool. Heat the oil and deep-fry the vegetarian tortoise briefly. Remove from the oil.

❸ Pour off all but 2 tablespoons of the oil. Fry the minced celery and minced ginger root briefly. Add ① and bring to a boil. Add the vegetarian tortoise, bamboo shoots, and carrots, and braise for 5 minutes, covered. Thicken with ②. Top with the blanched Chinese peapods and 1 tablespoon hot oil before transferring to a serving dish.

6人份
SERVES 6

麻婆豆腐

Spicy Szechuan Bean Curd

材料：

豆腐	1塊	辣豆瓣醬	1小匙
香菇	10公克(約五朵)	① ⎧ 高湯	1½杯
豆支	10公克	⎪ 醬油、麻油各	1大匙
芹菜末	1大匙	⎨ 味精	1小匙
香菜末	1大匙	⎩ 糖	½小匙
花椒粉	少許	② ⎧ 水	1大匙
油	2大匙	⎩ 太白粉	1小匙

❶豆腐切1公分立方(圖一)，香菇泡軟去蒂，豆支泡軟均切碎備用。

❷鍋熱入油2大匙，爆香芹菜末後，入香菇末、豆支末及辣豆瓣醬一起炒香，再入豆腐及①料(圖二)，煮至豆腐入味(約5分鐘)最後入②料勾芡盛盤，灑上花椒粉及香菜末即成。

INGREDIENTS:

1 cake	bean curd (*tofu*)
10 g (⅓ oz.)	dried Chinese black mushrooms
10 g (⅓ oz.)	dried pressed bean curd strips
1 T.	minced Chinese celery
1 T.	minced fresh coriander
pinch	ground Szechuan pepper (*hua chiao*)
2 T.	oil
1 t.	hot bean paste
① ⎧ 1½ c.	vegetarian stock
⎨ 1 T. each:	soy sauce, sesame oil
⎩ ½ t.	sugar
② ⎧ 1 T.	water
⎩ 1 t.	cornstarch

❶ Cut the bean curd into 1 cm (⅜″) cubes (illus. 1). Soak the dried mushrooms until soft and remove the stems. Soak the dried pressed bean curd strips until soft and mince.

❷ Heat a wok and add 2 tablespoons oil. Fry the minced Chinese celery briefly. Add the minced black mushroom, minced dried pressed bean curd strips, and the hot bean paste, and stir-fry briefly. Next add the bean curd and ① (illus. 2) and cook until the bean curd has absorbed the other flavors (about 5 minutes). Finally add ② to thicken. Transfer to a serving dish, sprinkle on some ground Szechuan pepper and minced fresh coriander, and serve.

6人份
SERVES 6

當歸大補湯

材料：

香菇頭…………	120公克	①	蛋 ……………	1個
當歸……………	6片		玉米粉………	1大匙
蓮子…………	30公克	②	酒…………	1大匙
紅棗…………	10個		麻油………	1小匙
枸杞…………	5公克		塩、味精…各¼小匙	
桂皮…………	少許	③	水…………	5杯
炸油…………	3杯		酒…………	1大匙
			味精、塩…各½小匙	

❶香菇頭泡軟拍碎，入①、②料拌勻(圖一)，分成12
　等份，擠成橄欖狀之香菇丸子(圖二)。

❷油3杯燒熱，將香菇丸子入鍋炸黃撈起備用。

❸燉鍋入炸好之香菇丸子、當歸、蓮子、紅棗、枸杞、
　桂皮及③料燉30分鐘即成。

6人份
SERVES 6

Chinese Tonic Soup

INGREDIENTS:

120 g (¼ lb.)		dried Chinese black mushroom stems
6 slices		Chinese angelica (*tang kuei*)
30 g (1 oz.)		lotus seeds
10		dried Chinese red dates
5 g (⅙ oz.)		Chinese wolfberry seeds (*kou chi tzu*)
1 stick		cinnamon
3 c.		oil for frying
①	1	egg
	1 T.	cornstarch
②	1 T.	rice wine
	1 t.	sesame oil
	¼ t.	salt
③	5 c.	water
	1 T.	rice wine
	½ t.	salt

❶ Soak the dried Chinese black mushroom stems until
soft, then pound with a meat mallet until well
chopped. Mix in ① and ② (illus. 1). Divide into 12
equal portions, and form each firmly into an olive
shape (illus. 2).

❷ Heat 3 cups oil. Deep-fry the mushroom balls until
golden and remove.

❸ Place the fried mushroom balls in a stew pot
together with the Chinese angelica, lotus seeds, red
dates, Chinese wolfberry seeds, stick cinnamon,
and ③. Stew 30 minutes and serve.

柑杞燉鰻

Eel Stewed With Black Dates

材料：

豆包·············	300公克	薑片·············	30公克
金菇·············	20公克	① { 味精·············	½小匙
香菇·············	10公克	塩·············	¼小匙
豆腐皮、紫菜···	各3張	胡椒粉·········	少許
蛋·············	1個	② { 水·············	5杯
黑棗·············	40公克	酒·············	2大匙
枸杞·············	5公克	塩·············	1小匙
當歸·············	3片	味精·············	¼小匙

❶香菇泡軟去蒂，金菇洗淨去頭切絲備用。

❷豆包切細絲與蛋、金菇、香菇絲及①料拌勻成餡，分成3份，每張豆腐皮上放紫菜1張、餡1份(圖一)，捲成長條(圖二)，以大火蒸5分鐘取出，將每條切成4等份是爲素鰻。

❸炸油4杯燒熱，素鰻入鍋炸黃撈起備用。

❹燉鍋入素鰻、黑棗、枸杞、當歸、薑片及②料燉20分鐘即成。

INGREDIENTS:

300 g (⅔ lb.)	bean curd pockets
20 g (⅔ oz.)	*enoki* (golden mushrooms)
10 g (⅓ oz.)	dried Chinese black mushrooms
3 sheets each:	bean curd skin, purple laver (*nori*)
1	egg
40 g (1½ oz.)	dried Chinese black dates (or substitute prunes)
5 g (⅙ oz.)	Chinese wolfberry seeds (*kou chi tzu*)
3 slices	Chinese angelica (*tang kuei*)
30 g (1 oz.)	ginger root slices
① { ¼ t.	salt
pinch	pepper
② { 5 c.	water
2 T.	rice wine
1 t.	salt

❶ Soak the mushrooms until soft, remove the stems, and cut into julienne strips. Wash the *enoki* and trim off the tough ends.

❷ Cut the bean curd pockets into fine strips. Combine with the egg, *enoki*, mushroom strips, and ① to make the filling. Divide into 3 portions. Place one sheet purple laver on each sheet of bean curd skin. Put one portion of filling on each (illus. 1) and roll into a cylinder (illus. 2). Steam 5 minutes over high heat. Cut each roll into 4 pieces. This is the vegetarian eel.

❸ Heat 3 cups oil. Deep-fry the vegetarian eel until golden and remove from oil.

❹ Place the vegetarian eel, Chinese black dates, Chinese wolfberry seeds, Chinese angelica, ginger root slices and ② in a stew pot. Stew 20 minutes and serve.

6人份
SERVES 6

酸菜肚片湯

Tripe and Pickled Greens Soup

材料：

酸菜·············· 170公克	香菇·················· 1朵		
胡蘿蔔···········20公克	①	太白粉········ 1小匙	
豌豆················ 8片		蛋白·············½個	
素豬肚·············· 1個		塩、味精···各¼小匙	
鮑魚菇············70公克	②	味精、塩···各 1小匙	
熟筍片············40公克		麻油·············1小匙	
素肉片············10公克		白醋·········½小匙	
		高湯············· 6杯	

❶酸菜洗淨切片，胡蘿蔔煮熟切片，豌豆去老梗燙熟，素豬肚、鮑魚菇均切與酸菜片同大小之斜片（圖一）備用。

❷素肉片以溫水泡軟擠去水份，入①料醃10分鐘，再以開水川燙後漂冷水瀝乾；香菇泡軟在上面刻“ㄨ”花狀備用。

❸扣碗中央排入香菇（圖二），將所有材料放入壓緊後以大火蒸10分鐘，倒在大碗中備用。

❹②料燒開，淋在❸料上即成。

INGREDIENTS:

170 g (6 oz.)	pickled mustard greens
20 g (⅔ oz.)	carrot
8	Chinese peapods
1 piece	vegetarian pork tripe
70 g (2½ oz.)	abalone mushrooms
40 g (1½ oz.)	cooked bamboo shoot slices
10 g (⅓ oz.)	vegetarian pork slices
1	dried Chinese black mushroom
① { 1 t.	cornstarch
½	egg white
¼ t.	salt
② { 1 t. each:	salt, sesame oil
½ t.	rice vinegar
6 c.	vegetarian stock

❶ Wash the pickled mustard greens and slice. Cook the carrot until done and slice. Remove the ends and strings from the Chinese peapods and blanch briefly in boiling water. Cut the vegetarian pork tripe and abalone mushrooms at an angle into pieces about the same size and shape as the pickled mustard greens (illus. 1).

❷ Soak the vegetarian pork slices in warm water until soft, then squeeze out the excess moisture. Marinate 10 minutes in ①. Blanch briefly in boiling water, cool in tap water, and drain well. Soak the dried mushroom until soft, then carve a ✳ shape onto the top.

❸ Place the black mushroom in a bowl (illus. 2), then arrange all the other ingredients in the bowl, pressing them down firmly. Steam 10 minutes over high heat. Transfer to a larger bowl.

❹ Bring ② to a boil, pour over the ingredients from step ❸, and serve.

6 人份
SERVES 6

柴把吉湯

Chicken Bundle Soup

材料：

綠竹筍	淨重90公克	薑	2片(切絲)
酸菜	50公克	炸油	2杯
香菇	12公克	水	3½杯
干瓢	12公克	① 塩、白醋	各 1小匙
金針	7公克	酒、麻油	各 1小匙
麵腸	80公克	味精	½小匙

❶ 綠竹筍煮熟，待涼與酸菜均切0.5×4公分長段；香菇、干瓢、金針均泡軟，香菇切0.5公分寬段，干瓢切10公分長段(圖一)，金針去頭均備用。

❷ 麵腸切0.5×4公分長段，炸油燒熱將麵腸炸金黃色撈起備用。

❸ 上述材料各取 1 份，再用干瓢綁緊成死結即成柴把(圖二)。

❹ 水燒開後入柴把及①料，待滾後入薑絲再煮 1 分鐘即成。

INGREDIENTS:

90 g (3½ oz.)	fresh bamboo shoots (net wt.)
50 g (1¾ oz.)	Chinese pickled mustard cabbage
12 g (⅖ oz.)	dried Chinese black mushrooms
12 g (⅖ oz.)	*kampyō* (dried gourd shavings)
7 g (¼ oz.)	dried lily buds
80 g (3 oz.)	vegetarian (wheat gluten) sausage
2 slices	ginger root, shredded
2 c.	oil for frying
3½ c.	water
	salt, rice vinegar, rice wine
① 1 t. each:	sesame oil

❶ Cook the fresh bamboo shoots until done, then allow to cool. Cut the bamboo shoots and pickled mustard cabbage into 0.5×4 cm (¼″×1½″) pieces. Soak the dried mushrooms, gourd shavings, and dried lily buds until soft. Cut the mushrooms into 0.5 cm (¼″) wide strips and the gourd shavings into 10 cm (4″) lengths (illus. 1). Cut the tough ends off the dried lily buds.

❷ Cut the vegetarian sausage into 0.5×4 cm (¼″×1½″) pieces. Heat the oil and deep-fry the vegetarian sausage until golden. Remove from the oil.

❸ Place one piece of each of the above ingredients into a pile, and tie it together tightly (make a double knot) with a length of the dried gourd shaving. This is a "bundle" (illus. 2). Repeat until the ingredients are used up.

❹ Bring the water to a boil, then add the "bundles" and ①. Add the shredded ginger root after the soup comes to a second boil. Cook for 1 minute. Serve.

6 人份
SERVES 6

三絲髮菜羹

Hair Seaweed Soup

材料：

髮菜⋯⋯⋯⋯⋯⋯ 7公克	高湯⋯⋯⋯⋯⋯⋯⋯ 4杯
筍⋯⋯⋯⋯⋯⋯⋯90公克	
香菇⋯⋯⋯⋯⋯⋯15公克	烏醋⋯⋯⋯⋯⋯ 3大匙
胡蘿蔔⋯⋯⋯⋯⋯50公克	酒、麻油⋯各 1大匙
金菇⋯⋯⋯⋯⋯⋯70公克	① 醬油⋯⋯⋯⋯ ½大匙
青豆仁⋯⋯⋯⋯⋯25公克	塩、味精⋯各 1小匙
菜酥⋯⋯⋯⋯⋯⋯少許	糖⋯⋯⋯⋯⋯⋯ 1小匙
油⋯⋯⋯⋯⋯⋯ 2大匙	胡椒粉⋯⋯⋯⋯少許
	② 水⋯⋯⋯⋯⋯ 3大匙
	太白粉⋯⋯⋯ 3小匙

❶髮菜泡水洗淨（圖一），竹筍煮熟切絲，香菇泡軟去蒂切絲，胡蘿蔔切絲，金菇去頭，青豆仁煮熟均備用。

❷鍋熱入油２大匙，爆香香菇絲、金菇，再入筍絲、胡蘿蔔絲、髮菜、高湯及①料煮開後，以②料勾芡，灑上菜酥及青豆仁即成（圖二）。

INGREDIENTS:

7 g (¼ oz.)	hair seaweed (fa tsai)
90 g (3 ½ oz.)	bamboo shoots
15 g (½ oz.)	dried Chinese black mushrooms
50 g (1¾ oz.)	carrot
70 g (2½ oz.)	enoki (golden mushrooms)
25 g (1 oz.)	peas
	vegetable crisp (tsai su), as desired
2 T.	oil
4 c.	vegetarian stock
① 3 T.	Chinese dark vinegar
1 T. each:	rice wine, sesame oil
½ T.	soy sauce
1 t. each:	salt, sugar
pinch	pepper
② 3 T.	water
3 t.	cornstarch

❶ Soak the hair seaweed briefly in water, then rinse clean (illus. 1). Cook the bamboo shoots until done, then cut into julienne strips. Soak the dried Chinese black mushrooms until soft, remove the stems, and cut into julienne strips. Cut the carrot into julienne strips. Trim the tough ends off the enoki. Cook the peas until done.

❷ Heat a wok and add 2 tablespoons oil. Fry the mushroom and enoki briefly, then add the bamboo shoots, carrot, hair seaweed, vegetarian stock, and ①, and bring to a boil. Thicken with ②, then sprinkle on some vegetable crisp and the peas. Serve (illus. 2).

6人份
SERVES 6

湯泡魚生

材料：

洋生菜	100公克	花生粉	1大匙
油條	1條	① 塩、味精	各1小匙
粉皮	½張	胡椒粉	少許
蒟蒻	1塊	高湯	6杯
香菜	少許	炸油	6杯

❶炸油燒熱，將油條炸脆切1公分小段，洋生菜洗淨切細絲，粉皮切1公分寬，蒟蒻切薄片均備用。

❷大碗中依序入洋生菜、粉皮、油條、蒟蒻片（圖一），最後灑上①料備用。

❸高湯燒開倒入大碗中（圖二），再灑上香菜即成。

Fish Slice Soup

INGREDIENTS:

100 g (3½ oz.)	head lettuce
1	Chinese fried cruller (*you-tiao*)
½	mung bean sheet (*fen pi*)
1 cake	*konnyaku*
	fresh coriander leaves, as desired
① 1 T.	peanut powder
1 t.	salt
pinch	pepper
6 c.	vegetarian stock
6 c.	oil for frying

❶ Heat the oil and fry the fried cruller until crisp. Cut into 1 cm (⅜″) pieces. Wash the lettuce and shred. Cut the mung bean sheet into 1 cm (⅜″) wide strips. Cut the *konnyaku* into thin slices.

❷ Arrange the following ingredients, in order, in a large bowl: shredded lettuce, mung bean sheet strips, fried cruller, *konnyaku* slices (illus. 1). Sprinkle on ① last.

❸ Bring the vegetarian stock to a boil and pour into the bowl (illus. 2). Garnish by sprinkling some fresh coriander leaves over the top, and serve.

6人份
SERVES 6

梅菜苦瓜湯

材料：

苦瓜	600公克	①	太白粉	1½大匙
炸好的豆包	1個		糖	½小匙
香菇	12公克		塩、味精	¼小匙
玉米筍	50公克	②	素高湯	5杯
洋菇	50公克		塩、糖	各1小匙
綠竹筍	50公克		味精	½小匙
梅干菜	60公克(1結)		酒	少許

❶香菇泡軟去蒂與豆包、玉米筍、洋菇、竹筍均切末，入①料拌成餡備用。

❷苦瓜去蒂頭切3公分寬段(圖一)並去籽，將餡塞入其中(圖二)，以大火蒸5分鐘取出備用。

❸梅干菜洗淨切末與苦瓜及②料同入圓盅內，以大火蒸20分鐘即成。

■若買不到已炸好的豆包，可買未炸的豆包自己先炸一下也可。

6人份

Stuffed Bitter Melon Soup

INGREDIENTS:

	600 g (1⅓ lb.)	bitter melon (balsam pear; *foo gwa; ku kua*)
	1	fried bean curd pocket
	12 g (⅖ oz.)	dried Chinese black mushrooms
	50 g (1¾ oz.)	baby corn
	50 g (1¾ oz.)	fresh mushrooms
	50 g (1¾ oz.)	bamboo shoots
	60 g (2 oz.)	dried mustard green (*mei kan tsai*)
①	1½ T.	cornstarch
	½ t.	sugar
	¼ t.	salt
②	5 c.	vegetarian stock
	1 t. each:	salt, sugar
	dash	rice wine

❶ Soak the dried Chinese black mushrooms until soft and remove the stems. Mince the black mushrooms, fried bean curd pocket, baby corn, fresh mushrooms, and bamboo shoots. Mix in ① to make a filling.

❷ Cut the stem off the bitter melon. Cut into 3 cm (1¼") rounds (illus. 1) and remove the seeds. Stuff the bitter melon rounds with the filling (illus. 2). Steam 5 minutes over high heat. Remove from the steamer.

❸ Wash the dried mustard greens thoroughly and mince. Place in a deep round porcelain dish together with the stuffed bitter melon and ②. Steam 20 minutes over high heat. Serve.

Note: If you cannot find bean curd pockets that have been pre-deep-fried, buy fresh and deep-fry them briefly yourself.

SERVES 6

蓮池生藕

Lotus Root Soup

材料：

| 蓮藕 | 200公克 |
| 生蓮子 | 60公克 |

① { 水 …………… 3杯
     塩 ………… 1小匙

② { 素高湯 ………… 5杯
     塩 ………… 1小匙
     糖、味精…各½小匙
     酒 ……………… 少許

❶ 蓮藕洗淨切0.5公分片狀(圖一)，以①料泡５分鐘後取出備用。

❷ 將蓮子、蓮藕及②料放入大碗中(圖二)，以大火蒸40分鐘即成。

■可用乾蓮子½杯代替生蓮子，但需先浸水半小時。

INGREDIENTS:

| 200 g (7 oz.) | fresh lotus root |
| 60 g (2 oz.) | fresh lotus seeds |

① { 3 c.   water
     1 t.   salt

② { 5 c.   vegetarian stock
     1 t.   salt
     ½ t.   sugar
     dash   rice wine

❶ Wash the lotus root thoroughly and pare. Cut into 0.5 cm (¼″) thick rounds (illus. 1). Soak in ① for 5 minutes and remove.

❷ Place the lotus seeds, lotus root, and ② in a large bowl (illus. 2). Steam 40 minutes over high heat. Serve.

Note: You may use ½ cup dried lotus seeds as a substitute for the fresh lotus seeds. Soak for ½ hour before use.

菠菜豆腐羹

Bean Curd and Spinach Soup

材料：

菠菜············ 200公克		素高湯·········· 5杯
嫩豆腐··············· 1塊	①	塩、味精···各 1小匙
筍片 (2×3公分)···50公克		胡椒粉·········少許
素火腿片 (2×3公分)·····	②	水·············· 3大匙
···········50公克		太白粉········ 1大匙
		麻油·············· 1小匙

❶ 菠菜洗淨去頭切細末，嫩豆腐切3×2×1公分小塊備用。

❷ ①料煮沸入筍片、豆腐，待再沸騰時，以②料勾芡（圖一），再入菠菜與火腿片拌勻（圖二），關火，起鍋前灑上麻油即成。

INGREDIENTS:

200 g (7 oz.)		fresh spinach
1 cake		soft bean curd (*tofu*)
50 g (1¾ oz.)		bamboo shoots (cut in 2×3 cm or ¾″ × 1¼″ slices)
50 g (1¾ oz.)		vegetarian ham (cut in 2×3 cm or ¾″ × 1¼″ slices)
①	5 c.	vegetarian stock
	1 t.	salt
	pinch	pepper
②	3 T.	water
	1 T.	cornstarch
1 t.		sesame oil

❶ Wash the fresh spinach thoroughly, trim off the stems, and mince finely. Cut the soft bean curd into 3×2×1 cm (1¼″ × ¾' × ⅜″) cubes.

❷ Bring ① to a boil, then add the bamboo shoots and bean curd. After the mixture comes to a second boil, thicken with ② (illus. 1). Stir in the spinach and vegetarian ham slices (illus. 2). Turn off the heat. Sprinkle the sesame oil over the top and serve.

6人份
SERVES 6

砂鍋素魚

材料：

素魚 ················· 1條	辣椒 ················· 4段
大白菜 ·········· 300公克	薑 ··················· 3片
豆腐 ··················· 1塊	
紅蘿蔔 ·········· 80公克	素高湯 ··········· 5杯
素蝦仁 ·········· 70公克	黑醋 ······· 1½大匙
冬粉 ······ 25公克(半把)	① 麻油 ··········· 1大匙
芹菜(5公分段) ····· 6段	塩、味精 ·· 各 1小匙
	胡椒粉、糖 ··· 各少許

❶ 素魚切1公分斜片勿斷，炸油燒7分熱(約300°F)，將素魚炸成金黃色撈起瀝油備用。

❷ 大白菜洗淨切3公分長段，豆腐切3×2×1公分長方塊，紅蘿蔔去皮切2×3公分片狀，冬粉泡軟均備用。

❸ 鍋熱入油2大匙，爆香薑片、辣椒段，即入大白菜及紅蘿蔔拌炒數下，再入①料煮沸；後入素魚、豆腐及素蝦仁。

❹ 砂鍋燒熱，將❸料倒入砂鍋內，再入芹菜段及冬粉，關火，蓋上鍋蓋燜2分鐘即成。

■ 若無法買到素蝦仁，可以自己製作，其製法如下：

材料：

蒟蒻粉 ············· 20公克	
	鹼粉 ·········· 10公克
①	水 ·············· 1杯
	紅蘿蔔泥 ······· ½杯

❶ 蒟蒻粉與①料拌勻(圖一)成糰，分成20等份，將每等份捏成蝦形(圖二)，入蒸籠以大火蒸8分鐘，取出川燙即為成品(圖三)。

Fish Chafing Dish

INGREDIENTS:

1	whole vegetarian fish
300 g (⅔ lb.)	Chinese cabbage
1 cake	bean curd
80 g (3 oz.)	carrot
70 g (2½ oz.)	vegetarian shrimp
25 g (1 oz.; ½ bunch)	bean thread (fun see; saifun)
6 pieces	Chinese celery (5 cm or 2″ long)
4 pieces	chili pepper
3 slices	ginger root
① 5 c.	vegetarian stock
1½ T.	Chinese dark vinegar
1 T.	sesame oil
1 t.	salt
pinch each:	pepper, sugar

❶ Slash the vegetarian fish at 1 cm (½″) intervals; do *not* cut all the way through. Heat oil for frying to about 300°F (149°C). Deep-fry the vegetarian fish until golden, remove, and drain.

❷ Wash the Chinese cabbage thoroughly, then cut into 3 cm (1¼″) pieces. Cut the bean curd into 3×2×1 cm (1¼″×¾″×⅜″) pieces. Pare the carrot and cut into 2×3 cm (¾″×1¼″) slices. Soak the bean thread until soft.

❸ Heat a wok and add 2 tablespoons oil. Fry the ginger root slices and chili pepper briefly, then add the Chinese cabbage and carrot, and stir-fry briefly. Add ① and bring to a boil. Add the vegetarian fish, bean curd, and vegetarian shrimp.

❹ Heat a clay pot and add the ingredients from step ❸. Add the celery and bean thread, turn off the heat, cover, and leave undisturbed for 2 minutes. Serve.

Note: If vegetarian shrimp are unavailable, use the following recipe to make your own.

Ingredients:

20 g (¾ oz.) konnyaku powder	
① 1 T. (⅓ oz.)	baking soda
1 c.	water
½ c.	carrot puree

Mix the *konnyaku* powder with ① (illus. 1) until smooth. Divide into 20 equal portions, and form each into the shape of a shrimp (illus. 2). Steam 8 minutes over high heat. Remove from the steamer, blanch briefly in boiling water, and they are ready for use in recipes calling for vegetarian shrimp (illus. 3).

四色燒賣

材料：

燒賣皮或水餃皮……12張
高麗菜………… 150公克
白豆干……50公克（½塊）
香菇末……………⅓杯
芹菜末、薑末…各 1大匙
毛豆末 ⎫
紅蘿蔔末 ⎬………各⅓杯
香菇末 ⎫
筍末 ⎬…………各⅓杯

① ⎰ 麻油………… 1小匙
　 ⎱ 味精………… ½小匙
　 ⎰ 塩、胡椒粉……少許

❶高麗菜洗淨切末，以½大匙塩醃泡5分鐘，擠掉水份備用。
❷白豆干洗淨切末，與香菇末、芹菜末、薑末及高麗菜末，入①料拌勻成餡，再分成12等份備用。
❸將每份餡以燒賣皮包成四角燒賣形（圖一）；再分別以毛豆、紅蘿蔔、香菇、筍末在四角的空隙地方裝飾之（圖二），後入蒸籠大火蒸10分鐘即成。

Four-Color Shao Mai

INGREDIENTS:

12	*shao mai* or *shui chiao* (boiled dumpling) flour wrappers
150 g (⅓ lb.)	cabbage
50 g (1¾ oz.; ½ piece)	white pressed bean curd (*tou kan*)
⅓ c.	minced dried Chinese black mushroom (soak first)
1 T. each:	minced Chinese celery, minced ginger root
⅓ c. each:	minced cooked fresh soybeans, minced carrot, minced dried Chinese black mushrooms, minced bamboo shoots
① ⎰ 1 t. ⎱ pinch each:	sesame oil / salt, pepper

❶ Wash the cabbage and mince finely. Sprinkle ½ tablespoon salt over it and leave undisturbed for 5 minutes. Squeeze out the excess moisture.

❷ Wash the white pressed bean curd and mince. Mix ① into the minced pressed bean curd, minced black mushroom, minced Chinese celery, minced ginger root, and minced cabbage to make the filling. Divide into 12 equally-sized portions.

❸ Stuff the *shao mai* flour wrappers with the filling, forming four "pockets" (illus. 1). Decorate the top of each pocket with minced fresh soybean, carrot, black mushroom, and bamboo shoots, respectively (illus. 2). Steam 10 minutes over high heat, and serve.

6人份
SERVES 6

八寶芋泥

Eight-Treasure Taro Paste

材料：

芋頭…………… 300公克	
蜜棗…………… 50公克	① 糖………………½杯
桔餅…………… 50公克	油……………… 1大匙
冬瓜糖………… 50公克	② 水……………… 1杯
罐頭鳳梨……… 2片	奶水………… 1大匙
葡萄乾………… 20公克	糖…………… 1小匙
黃豆沙………… 80公克	太白粉……… 1小匙

❶芋頭去皮切片蒸熟，取出與①料拌成泥，再分成二
等份備用。

❷桔餅、冬瓜糖、鳳梨均切大丁備用。

❸蜜棗、桔餅、冬瓜糖、鳳梨、葡萄乾依序排入扣碗
內（圖一），其上置一份芋泥並壓緊（圖二），再入黃
豆沙及剩餘之芋泥並壓緊，續以大火蒸20分鐘即取
出倒扣盤中。

❹②料拌勻煮開淋在八寶芋泥上即成。

■此道甜點的材料可隨個人喜好加以變化。

INGREDIENTS:

300 g (⅔ lb.)	taros
50 g (1¾ oz.)	preserved Chinese black dates
50 g (1¾ oz.)	candied kumquats
50 g (1¾ oz.)	winter melon candy
2 slices	canned pineapple
20 g (¾ oz.)	raisins
80 g (3 oz.)	yellow mung bean paste
① ½ c.	sugar
1 T.	oil
② 1 c.	water
1 T.	milk
1 t.	sugar
1 t.	cornstarch

❶ Peel the taros, slice, and steam until soft. Mash together
with ① into a smooth paste. Divide into 2 equal portions.

❷ Cut the candied kumquat, winter melon candy, and
pineapple into cubes.

❸ Arrange the preserved Chinese black dates, candied
kumquat, winter melon candy, pineapple, and raisins, in
order, in a bowl (illus. 1). Cover with a layer of taro paste
and press down firmly (illus. 2). On top of that place the
yellow mung bean paste, and then the remaining taro
paste, again pressing down firmly. Steam 20 minutes over
high heat. Invert the bowl onto a plate.

❹ Mix ② until blended and bring to a boil. Pour over the
taro paste and serve.

Note: The ingredients in this dessert may be varied according
to personal preference.

6人份
SERVES 6

炸春捲

Vegetarian Spring Rolls

材料：

春捲皮‥‥‥‥‥‥‥12張
銀芽‥‥‥‥‥‥ 100公克
素肉絲‥‥‥‥‥‥80公克
香菇絲‥‥‥‥‥‥80公克
紅蘿蔔絲‥‥‥‥‥50公克
筍絲‥‥‥‥‥‥‥50公克
芹菜段（每段 3公分） 6段
炸油‥‥‥‥‥‥‥‥ 6杯

① { 麵粉‥‥‥‥‥ 1大匙
  { 水‥‥‥‥‥‥ 1大匙

② { 醬油‥‥‥‥‥ 1小匙
  { 麻油‥‥‥‥‥ 1小匙
  { 塩、味精‥‥各¼小匙
  { 糖‥‥‥‥‥‥‥¼小匙

❶①料拌勻成麵糊備用。
❷鍋燒熱入油２大匙，爆香芹菜段，加入素肉絲、香菇絲、紅蘿蔔絲、筍絲及銀芽（圖一），拌炒數下，再入②料拌勻即盛盤分成12等份的餡備用。
❸每張春捲皮包１份餡捲成圓筒狀（圖二），接口以麵糊粘緊，一共包成12條春捲。
❹炸油燒８分熱（約350°F），入春捲炸成金黃色撈起瀝油即成。

INGREDIENTS:

12	spring roll wrappers
100 g (3½ oz.)	mung bean sprouts (both ends removed)
80 g (3 oz.) each:	vegetarian meat shreds, julienned dried Chinese black mushroom
50 g (1¾ oz.) each:	julienned carrot, julienned bamboo shoots
6 pieces	Chinese celery (3 cm or 1¼" each)
6 c.	oil for frying
① { 1 T. { 1 T.	flour water
② { 1 t. each: { ¼ t. each:	soy sauce, sesame oil salt, sugar

❶ Mix ① into a smooth batter.
❷ Heat a wok and add 2 tablespoons oil. Fry the celery briefly. Add the vegetarian meat shreds, black mushroom, carrot, bamboo shoots, and mung bean sprouts (illus. 1), and stir-fry briefly. Add ②, combine well, and transfer to a plate. Divide into 12 equal portions of filling.
❸ Wrap one portion of filling in each spring roll wrapper, forming a cylindrical shape (illus. 2). Seal tightly with a little batter.
❹ Heat the oil to about 350°F (177°C). Deep-fry the spring rolls until golden. Remove from the oil, drain, and serve.

6人份
SERVES 6

透明水晶包

Crystal Balls

材料：

紅豆沙………… 150公克
太白粉…………… 1杯
① { 熱開水…………¾杯
    油……………½大匙

❶豆沙分成12等份揉圓備用。

❷①料攪拌均勻，徐徐倒入太白粉揉成麵糰，再分成
12等份，每份麵糰以擀麵棍擀成直徑5公分圓的麵
皮（圖一），再將每份豆沙包在麵皮內（圖二），入蒸
籠以大火蒸8分鐘即成。

INGREDIENTS:

150 g (⅓ lb.)	sweet red bean (*adzuki*) paste
1 c.	cornstarch
① { ¾ c.	hot water
½ T.	oil

❶ Divide the red bean paste into 12 equal portions, and roll into balls.

❷ Mix ①, then slowly pour in the cornstarch and knead into a dough. Divide into 12 equal portions. With a rolling pin, roll each portion of dough into a round dumpling wrapper 5 cm (2″) in diameter (illus. 1). Wrap a portion of red bean paste in each wrapper (illus. 2) and steam 8 minutes over high heat. Serve.

6人份
SERVES 6

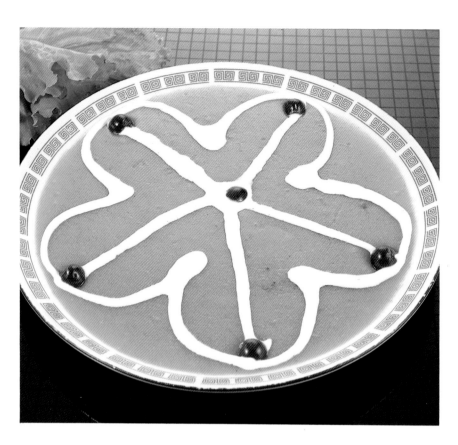

青豆鮮泥

Peas Royale

材料：
青豆罐頭········· 120公克
熟地瓜(去皮)··· 150公克
櫻桃···················· 3顆
鮮奶油················ 1杯
① { 水················· 2杯
　 { 糖·················⅔杯

❶青豆、地瓜與①料入果汁機打成泥狀，倒入鍋中煮成濃稠狀(圖一)，邊煮邊攪拌再盛盤備用。
❷鮮奶油以打蛋器打成泡沫狀(圖二)，裝飾在豆泥上，並以櫻桃點綴裝飾即成。

INGREDIENTS:
120 g (¼ lb.)	canned (or frozen) peas
150 g (⅓ lb.)	sweet potatoes, pared and cooked soft
3	maraschino cherries
1 c.	fresh whipping cream, sweetened
① { 2 c.	water
{ ⅔ c.	sugar

❶ Puree the peas, sweet potatoes, and ① in a blender. Pour into a saucepan and cook until thickened (illus. 1), stirring constantly. Transfer to a shallow bowl.
❷ Whip the cream with a whisk until frothy (illus. 2), and use it to garnish the pea and sweet potato paste. Top with the maraschino cherries and serve.

6人份
SERVES 6

蜜桃西谷米

Peach Tapioca Dessert

材料：

西谷米‥‥‥‥‥‥‥‥‥³⁄₄杯
水蜜桃罐頭‥‥‥‥‥‥ 1罐
水‥‥‥‥‥‥‥‥‥‥‥ 4杯
① { 冷開水‥‥‥‥‥ 1杯
糖‥‥‥‥‥‥‥‥½杯
奶水‥‥‥‥ 1½大匙

❶水4杯燒開入西谷米煮熟（圖一），撈起放入碗中待涼備用。
❷水蜜桃罐頭連汁一起倒入果汁機打成汁，並倒入碗中加①料拌勻，再入煮好的西谷米（圖二）拌勻即成。

INGREDIENTS:

³⁄₄ c.	pearl tapioca or pearl sago
1 can	cling peaches
4 c.	water
① { 1 c.	cold water
½ c.	sugar
1½ T.	milk

❶ Bring the 4 cups water to a boil, add the pearl tapioca, and cook until done (illus. 2). Drain, transfer to a bowl, and allow to cool.
❷ Pour the cling peaches together with syrup into a blender and puree. Pour into a bowl and mix with ①. Stir in the cooked tapioca (illus. 2) until blended, and serve.

6人份
SERVES 6

核桃糊

Sweet Walnut Soup

材料：
核桃⋯⋯⋯⋯⋯⋯⋯ 1杯
熱水⋯⋯⋯⋯⋯⋯⋯ 3杯
水⋯⋯⋯⋯⋯⋯⋯⋯ 2杯
① { 水⋯⋯⋯⋯⋯⋯⋯ 1杯
糖⋯⋯⋯⋯⋯⋯ 4大匙
糯米粉⋯⋯⋯⋯ 2大匙

❶核桃以３杯熱水泡40分鐘後，取出，加２杯水入果
汁機打成漿狀；再以篩網過濾（圖一）備用。

❷①料拌勻，與核桃漿入鍋同煮（圖二）８分鐘即成。

INGREDIENTS:

1 c.		walnuts
3 c.		hot water
2 c.		water
①	1 c.	water
	4 T.	sugar
	2 T.	glutinous ("sweet") rice flour (*mochi* flour)

❶ Soak the walnuts in 3 cups hot water for 40 minutes. Drain. Place in a blender with 2 cups water and puree. Strain (illus. 1) and set aside.

❷ Mix ① until blended. Add to a saucepan together with the walnut puree and cook (illus. 2) 8 minutes. Serve.

豆沙鍋餅

材料：
紅豆沙‥‥‥‥‥ 150公克
①{ 麵粉‥‥‥‥‥‥ 1杯
   蛋‥‥‥‥‥‥‥ 3個
   油‥‥‥‥‥‥‥ 3大匙

❶將①料調成麵糊，與豆沙分成二等份備用。
❷鍋熱入油1大匙及1份麵糊，以小火煎成直徑約15
公分的麵皮，取出再以同法煎第二張麵皮備用。
❸將1份紅豆沙放在1張麵皮中間，壓平成5公分寬
的長條(圖一)，再將左、右兩邊的麵皮對折成鍋餅
(圖二)，另一份亦同樣作法。
❹鍋熱入餘油1大匙，以小火將鍋餅煎成金黃色，取
出切成2×5公分長方形排盤即成。

6人份
SERVES 6

Red Bean Crêpes

INGREDIENTS:
150 g (⅓ lb.)   sweet red (*adzuki*) bean paste
①{ 1 c.   flour
   3   eggs
   3 T.   oil

❶ Mix ① into a smooth batter. Divide the sweet
bean paste into 2 equal portions.
❷ Heat a frying pan and add 1 tablespoon oil.
Pour in half of the batter and fry over low heat
into a crêpe 15 cm (6″) in diameter. Fry the
second half of the batter in the same way.
❸ Place one portion of red bean paste on one
of the crêpes and press it into a 5 cm (2″)
rectangular shape (illus. 1). Fold the two ends
over the top (illus. 2). Repeat for the remaining
portion of red bean paste and crêpe.
❹ Heat the frying pan and add 1 tablespoon oil.
Pan-fry the red bean paste crêpes until
golden. Remove and cut into 2×5 cm (¾″×2″)
strips. Arrange on a plate and serve.

生磨馬蹄泥

Sweet Water Chestnut Soup

材料：
荸薺‥‥‥‥‥‥ 300公克
櫻桃末‥‥‥‥‥‥ 3大匙
奶水‥‥‥‥‥‥‥ 2大匙
① { 清水‥‥‥‥‥‥ 3杯
　 { 糖‥‥‥‥‥‥‥ ½杯

❶荸薺與①料入果汁機內攪拌成泥狀 (圖一) 備用。
❷荸薺泥入鍋燒開，改小火，倒入奶水 (圖二) 拌勻，
　再盛入碗中灑上櫻桃末即成。

INGREDIENTS:
300 g (⅔ lb.)	water chestnuts, peeled
3 T.	minced maraschino cherries
2 T.	milk
① { 3 c.	water
{ ½ c.	sugar

❶ Put the water chestnuts and ① into a blender and puree (illus. 1).

❷ Pour the water chestnut puree into a saucepan and bring to a boil. Lower the heat and add the milk (illus. 2). Mix until well blended.Pour into a bowl and sprinkle the minced maraschino cherries over the top. Serve.

6人份
SERVES 6

Chin-Chin

5th fl., 125 Sung Chiang Rd, Taipe104 ,

純青出版社

劃撥帳號：12106299

電　話：（〇二）五〇七四九〇二・五〇八四三三一

地　址：台北市松江路125號5樓

微波食譜第一冊

- 62道菜
- 112頁
- 中英對照
- 平裝280元
  精裝300元

Microwave Cooking Chinese Style

- 62 recipes
- 112 pages
- Chinese/English Bilingual

微波食譜第二冊

- 76道菜
- 128頁
- 中英對照
- 平裝280元
  精裝330元

Microwave Cooking Chinese Style (II)

- 76 recipes
- 128 pages
- Chinese/English Bilingual

健康食譜

- 100道菜
- 120頁
- 中英對照
- 平裝280元

Healthful Cooking

- 100 recipes
- 120 pages
- Chinese/English Bilingual

台灣菜

- 73道菜
- 120頁
- 中英對照
- 平裝300元

Chinese Cuisine Taiwanese Style

- 73 recipes
- 120 pages
- Chinese/English Bilingual

四川菜

- 115道菜
- 96頁
- 中英對照
- 平裝300元

Chinese Cuisine Szechwan Style

- 115 recipes
- 96 pages
- Chinese/English Bilingual

上海菜

- 91道菜
- 96頁
- 中英對照
- 平裝300元

Chinese Cuisine Shanghai Style

- 91 recipes
- 96 pages
- Chinese/English Bilingual

Publishing

Taiwan, R.O.C. Tel : (02)507-4902

麵食-精華篇
- 87道菜
- 96頁
- 中英對照
- 平裝280元

Noodles
Classical Cooking
- 87 recipes
- 96 pages
- Chinese/English Bilingual

麵食-家常篇
- 91道菜
- 96頁
- 中英對照
- 平裝280元

Noodles
Home Cooking
- 91 recipes
- 96 pages
- Chinese/English Bilingual

米食-傳統篇
- 82道菜
- 96頁
- 中英對照
- 平裝280元

Rice
Traditional Cooking
- 82 recipes
- 96 pages
- Chinese/English Bilingual

米食-家常篇
- 84道菜
- 96頁
- 中英對照
- 平裝280元

Rice
Home Cooking
- 84 recipes
- 96 pages
- Chinese/English Bilingual

嬰幼兒食譜
- 140道菜
- 104頁
- 中文版
- 平裝250元

Baby & Children Cooking
- 140 recipes
- 104 pages
- Chinese

營養便當
- 147道菜
- 96頁
- 中文版
- 平裝250元

Lunch Box
- 147 recipes
- 96 pages
- Chinese

素食
- 84道菜
- 116頁
- 中英對照
- 平裝300元

Vegetarian Cooking
- 84 recipes
- 116 pages
- Chinese/English Bilingual

家常100
- 100道菜
- 96頁
- 中英對照
- 平裝280元

Favorite Chinese Dishes
- 100 recipes
- 96 pages
- Chinese/English Bilingual

味全家政班

味全家政班創立於民國五十年，經過三十餘年的努力，它不只是國內歷史最悠久的家政研習班，更成爲一所正式學制之外的專門學校。

創立之初，味全家政班以教授中國菜及研習烹飪技術爲主，因教學成果良好，備受各界讚譽，乃於民國五十二年，增闢插花、工藝、美容等各門專科，精湛的師資，教學內容的充實，深獲海內外的肯定與好評。

三十餘年來，先後來班參與研習的學員已近二十萬人次，學員的足跡遍及台灣以外，更有許多國外的團體或個人專程抵台，到味全家政班求教，在習得中國菜烹調的精髓後，或返回居住地經營餐飲業，或擔任家政教師，或獲聘爲中國餐廳主廚者大有人在，成就倍受激賞。

近年來，味全家政班亟力研究開發改良中國菜餚，並深入國際間，採集各種精緻、道地美食，除了樹立中華文化「食的精神」外，並將各國烹飪口味去蕪存菁，擷取地方特色。爲了確保這些研究工作更加落實，我們特將這些集合海內外餐飲界與研發單位的精典之作，以縝密的拍攝技巧與專業編輯，出版各式食譜，以做傳承。

薪傳與發揚中國烹飪的藝術，是味全家政班一貫的理念，日後，也將秉持宗旨，永續不輟。

Wei-Chuan Cooking School

Since its establishment in 1961, Wei-Chuan Cookin School has made a continuous commitment towar improving and modernizing the culinary art of cookin and special skills training. As a result, it is the olde and most successful school of its kind in Taiwan.

In the beginning, Wei-Chuan Cooking School wo primarily teaching and researching Chinese cookin techniques. However, due to popular demand, th curriculum was expanded to cover courese in flowe arrangements, handcrafts, beauty care, dress makin and many other specialized fields by 1963.

The fact that almost 200,000 students, from Taiwa and other countries all over the world, have matricu lated in this school can be directly attributed to the hig quality of the teaching staff and the excellent curricu lum provided to the studends. Many of the graduate have become successful restaurant owners and chef and in numerous cases, respected teachers.

While Wei-Chuan Cooking School has always bee committed to developing and improving Chinese cu sine, we have recently extended our efforts towar gathering information and researching recipes fro defferent provinces of China. With the same dedica tion to accuracy and perfection as always, we hav begun to publish these authentic regional gourm recipes for our devoted readers. These new publica tions will continue to reflect the fine tradition of quali our public has grown to appreciate and expect.

純青食譜　版權所有

局版台業字第3884號

印刷：中華彩色印刷股份有限公司

中華民國77年11月初版發行

中華民國84年1月七版發行

定價：平裝／新台幣參佰元整

　　　　精裝／新台幣參佰元整

Printer: China Color Printing Co., Inc.
First Printing, November,1988
Seventh Printing, January, 1995
ISBN : 0-941676-20-X